The Hidden Side of Bridge

Terence Reese
David Bird

B.T. Batsford Ltd, *London*

First published 1988
First Batsford edition 1996

ISBN 0 7134 7931 0
A CIP catalogue record for this book is available
from the British Library.

Printed by Redwood Books, Trowbridge, Wiltshire.

Published by B.T. Batsford Ltd,
4 Fitzhardinge Street,
London W1H 0AH

A Batsford Bridge Book
Series Editor: Tony Sowter.

CONTENTS

Foreword

It is easy, in the midst of the fray, to forget that bridge is a young, almost a new game. In its present form it has existed for about sixty years; not much to put against the thousands of years in which chess and backgammon have been played. Each of those games still, at expert level, varies its form every twenty years or so. It is hardly surprising that there is always something new to write about bridge.

This book deals mostly with forms of play that are not part of the usual game at present, but may well become so in the next few years. None of the hands (all right, one or two perhaps) is in the least fanciful; most are from recorded events where in many cases we have been able to give the names of the players.

1

When the 'normal' card is wrong

Sometimes, for several consecutive hands, it is quite good enough to switch to autopilot, pushing out the obvious cards and hoping that the opponents will fall over themselves. Every now and again, though, a hand comes along where the 'normal' card is not good enough.

Can you spot the error that declarer, a strong player, made on this deal?

```
Dealer South        ♠ 7 4 2
Love all            ♡ Q J 10 8
                    ◇ K J 6 5
                    ♣ Q 10
     ♠ 8 3                        ♠ A Q 10 9 5
     ♡ A 9 6 2                    ♡ K 7 4
     ◇ A 10 9 8                   ◇ 4 2
     ♣ 7 5 4                      ♣ 8 6 3
                    ♠ K J 6
                    ♡ 5 3
                    ◇ Q 7 3
                    ♣ A K J 9 2
```

South	West	North	East
1♣	No	1♡	1♠
1NT	No	3NT	End

West's lead of ♠ 8 ran to the queen and king, and at trick two declarer led a low diamond. West played a slightly deceptive 9, the jack won, and a diamond was returned to the queen and ace.

Judging the situation well, West did not play the expected spade, but established a second trick in diamonds. When declarer led a spade towards the king, East had his ace on the table in quick time. The defenders cashed two hearts and a diamond to defeat the contract.

Clearly declarer should not have allowed the defenders to establish two diamonds before he had scored his second spade trick. But what could he have done about it? It may seem a little odd that the *queen* of diamonds from hand at trick two would be safe against any defence. It might not work well if East had ◇ A 10 9 x and held off the first round, but West was more likely than East to hold the length in diamonds.

Perhaps the most common setting for the play of an 'unusual' card occurs in elimination play. The defender thrown on lead must consider carefully his choice of exit card. This deal is typical:

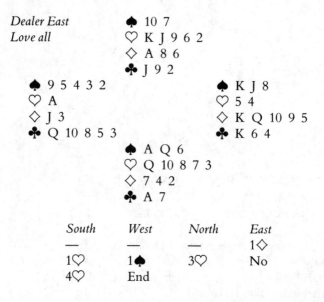

Dealer East	♠ 10 7		
Love all	♡ K J 9 6 2		
	◇ A 8 6		
	♣ J 9 2		

♠ 9 5 4 3 2		♠ K J 8
♡ A		♡ 5 4
◇ J 3		◇ K Q 10 9 5
♣ Q 10 8 5 3		♣ K 6 4

	♠ A Q 6		
	♡ Q 10 8 7 3		
	◇ 7 4 2		
	♣ A 7		

South	West	North	East
—	—	—	1◇
1♡	1♠	3♡	No
4♡	End		

West leads the jack of diamonds, which is allowed to hold. The next diamond is won in dummy and South prepares for a possible elimination by finessing the queen of spades, cashing the ace and ruffing a spade. Only then does he play a trump.

West, who would have been well advised to cash his ace of trumps earlier, wins the trick. He must find an exit in this end position:

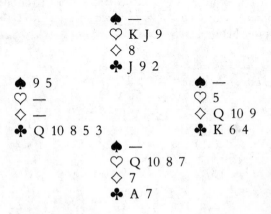

As you see, a low club will not be good enough. The 9 will force East's king, taken by the ace, and a second round of clubs will establish dummy's jack for a discard. West must lead the *queen* of clubs; then declarer will have no answer.

These elimination positions are frequently a setting for bluff and double-bluff. Imagine you have put West on lead and he has to open this diamond suit:

$$\diamondsuit \ J \ 9 \ 4$$

$\diamondsuit$ K led

$$\diamondsuit \ A \ 8 \ 5$$

When West leads the king, there are at least three possibilities. He may be a novice, playing what he regards as the natural card from KQ x (x). He may be a more experienced player, trying the king from K 10 x x. Or he may be a double-bluffer with KQ x x, hoping that you will read him for K 10 x x.

The same three possibilities are there when West exits with a low card. How you read the situation will depend on your opinion of his skill as a defender, and also on what you think his opinion is of you as a declarer!

Here is another deal where the defender has to choose an imaginative exit card. It was played in a Bermuda Bowl encounter between USA and Italy.

Dealer North ♠ A 10 8 7
East-West game ♡ J 8 3
◇ 10 3
♣ A 10 8 3

♠ J 4 3   ♠ K 5 2
♡ A 10 7 2   ♡ Q 9 5 4
◇ Q 5   ◇ K J 8 7
♣ J 9 4 2   ♣ K 5

♠ Q 9 6
♡ K 6
◇ A 9 6 4 2
♣ Q 7 6

South	West	North	East
Eisenberg	Garozzo	Hamilton	Franco
—	—	No	1◇
No	1♡	Dble	No
1♠	No	No	2♡
2♠(!)	End		

Eisenberg's two spade call may seem a strange effort, but he could be reasonably sure that his partner, a passed hand, would hold four spades.

West led a trump to his partner's king and another

4

trump was returned. When a low club was led from the dummy, East rose with the king and returned a third round of trumps.

South exited with a low diamond to West's queen and won the diamond return. After ruffing a diamond he re-entered his hand with the queen of clubs. This was the ending:

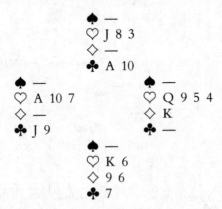

South, who had lost three tricks, had a reliable count and was confident of the club finesse. West was likely to hold the heart ace and Eisenberg thought of exiting with a diamond, to force a heart lead from East. But meanwhile, it seemed, he would be abandoning the club finesse. In the end he finessed ♣ 10, cashed the ace and lost the last three tricks, going one down.

It looks as though the diamond exit would have worked. West throws a heart and so does the dummy. When East leads a low heart South plays low and West is in a dilemma. If he plays low, a heart a returned and he has to lead into dummy's ♣ A 10. If instead he wins with ♡ A, South will gain the lead with ♡ K to take the club finesse.

But wait a moment. Suppose East, when thrown in, exits with the *queen* of hearts! This remarkable play saves the defence.

In the same vein is this striking deal, reported from the Olympiad in Biarritz. Try it as a defensive problem from the West seat.

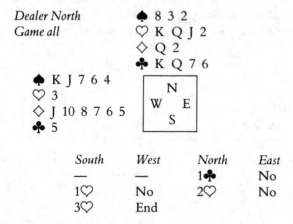

Dealer North ♠ 8 3 2
Game all ♡ K Q J 2
  ◇ Q 2
  ♣ K Q 7 6

♠ K J 7 6 4
♡ 3
◇ J 10 8 7 6 5
♣ 5

	N	
W		E
	S	

South	West	North	East
—	—	1♣	No
1♡	No	2♡	No
3♡	End		

You lead your singleton club. Partner wins with the ace and returns ♣ 8, on which South plays the jack. Partner's 8 appears to be a middle card, not inviting specifically a spade or a diamond. How should you play after ruffing the club return?

The jack of diamonds may seem the obvious card, but this will hardly lead to the five tricks needed to beat the contract. When you have made up your mind, look at the full deal:

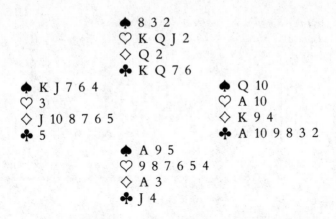

```
                    ♠ 8 3 2
                    ♡ K Q J 2
                    ♢ Q 2
                    ♣ K Q 7 6
♠ K J 7 6 4                         ♠ Q 10
♡ 3                                 ♡ A 10
♢ J 10 8 7 6 5                      ♢ K 9 4
♣ 5                                 ♣ A 10 9 8 3 2
                    ♠ A 9 5
                    ♡ 9 8 7 6 5 4
                    ♢ A 3
                    ♣ J 4
```

If you lead a diamond at trick 3 South will force out the ace of hearts and discard two spade losers on ♣ K Q. A low spade return after the club ruff will fare no better; declarer will win the second round and still make the contract.

According to a report in the French magazine *Le Bridgeur*, Michel Corn made the super play of the *jack* of spades. Now declarer is lost. If he wins he runs into a spade ruff, and if he ducks then West will switch to the jack of diamonds.

Some people always like to find something different, and French international Dominique Poubeau pointed out that the king of spades at trick 3 would also defeat the contract – always supposing that East dropped the queen!

If your own defence is not up to such a brilliant switch, don't worry. Next time the hand comes around you will have to content yourself with the cold vulnerable game in spades or diamonds.

By way of a change, here's a hand where a defender chooses an unorthodox card merely for the purpose of guiding partner's defence. The setting is the England–Switzerland match in the European Championships at Dun Laoghaire in Eire. The year? 1952!

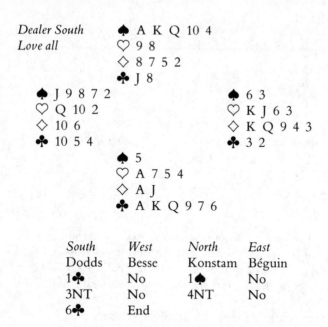

Dealer South　　　♠ A K Q 10 4
Love all　　　　　♡ 9 8
　　　　　　　　　◇ 8 7 5 2
　　　　　　　　　♣ J 8

♠ J 9 8 7 2　　　　　　　　　　　♠ 6 3
♡ Q 10 2　　　　　　　　　　　　♡ K J 6 3
◇ 10 6　　　　　　　　　　　　　◇ K Q 9 4 3
♣ 10 5 4　　　　　　　　　　　　♣ 3 2

　　　　　　　　　♠ 5
　　　　　　　　　♡ A 7 5 4
　　　　　　　　　◇ A J
　　　　　　　　　♣ A K Q 9 7 6

South	West	North	East
Dodds	Besse	Konstam	Béguin
1♣	No	1♠	No
3NT	No	4NT	No
6♣	End		

In the other room the same contract had failed on a diamond lead. Here, Besse tried his luck with ♠ 9.

Dodds put up dummy's ace and ran ♡ 9 to West's 10. Besse, with declarer's notrump rebid fresh in his mind, lost no time in returning a spade. Declarer could now ruff two hearts in the dummy, bringing his total to twelve. A trump switch would have left him a trick short.

It is possible to fault West (he was not familiar with Leslie Dodds's individual bidding style), but the player who really missed his chance was East. It would have been good play for him to go up with the king of hearts, or even the jack, at trick 3. This would indicate that he was not particularly anxious for West to gain the lead.

Less exotic than some of the previous plays, but perhaps of more practical importance, are the situations where a defender must unblock to avoid being endplayed. The

German international, Gynz, won a Bols brilliancy prize on this deal, where he was sitting West.

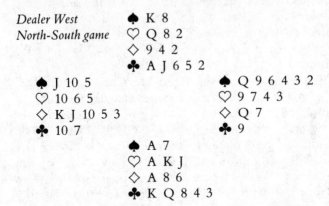

Dealer West
North-South game

♠ K 8
♡ Q 8 2
♢ 9 4 2
♣ A J 6 5 2

♠ J 10 5
♡ 10 6 5
♢ K J 10 5 3
♣ 10 7

♠ Q 9 6 4 3 2
♡ 9 7 4 3
♢ Q 7
♣ 9

♠ A 7
♡ A K J
♢ A 8 6
♣ K Q 8 4 3

Chemla, for France, played as South in six clubs. West led the jack of spades, won in dummy. After his usual two seconds' thought Chemla played a diamond to the ace, drew trumps, and eliminated the major suits. The lead was in the South hand with these cards remaining:

♠ —
♡ —
♢ 4 2
♣ A J 6

♠ 10
♡ —
♢ K J 10 5
♣ —

♠ Q 9 6
♡ 9
♢ Q
♣ —

♠ —
♡ —
♢ 8 6
♣ 8 4 3

When declarer led a diamond West played the 'Crocodile

Coup', opening his jaws to play the king and swallow his partner's queen. Had he played any other card East would have been left on play, forced to concede a ruff-and-discard.

Since the declarer would certainly not have led a diamond to the ace early on if he had held A Q, this defence was not too difficult; but what else strikes you about the hand?

First, it was very smart play for Chemla to lead the diamond at once, before opponents were likely to think of unblocking.

Second, it would have been fine play by East to go up with the queen on the first diamond lead, preventing any possibility of a throw-in. If South had held, say, A J x in diamonds, the unblock would have been essential. This play of the queen from Q x can hardly lose when dummy has low cards.

A final point is that East had another chance to dispose of the diamond queen when the second round of trumps was played.

As most players have discovered at one time or another, the defence is more likely to prosper when the high cards are divided between the two defenders than when they are concentrated in one hand. The feeble cry of 'I had to double, partner, I had 16 points' is less common than it used to be. West could not resist doubling on the following hand, but he had to defend like a demon to justify the call.

Dealer South	♠ K 10 8
North-South game	♡ K 4
	♢ A 8 7 5 4 2
	♣ Q 5

♠ A Q 6	♠ J 9 5 4 2
♡ Q J 9 2	♡ 8 7 6 3
♢ K J	♢ —
♣ K 10 6 2	♣ 9 8 7 4

	♠ 7 3
	♡ A 10 5
	♢ Q 10 9 6 3
	♣ A J 3

South	West	North	East
1♢	Dble	2NT	No
3♢	No	5♢	No
No	Dble	End	

North's 2 NT, over the double, promised diamond support. No doubt, he should have called 3 NT at his second turn. After a spade lead to West's queen he would make that contract by holding up the king.

However, the actual contract was five diamonds doubled and West's queen of hearts was won in dummy. Ace and another trump put West on lead. What should he play next?

A heart or a club will be fatal immediately. If instead West tries ace and another spade, declarer will ruff a spade, cash the ace of clubs and run dummy's trumps to squeeze West in hearts and clubs.

What else can West try? To exit with ♠ 6 would lead nowhere. West would have to win the next round of spades and the same squeeze in hearts and clubs would result. So, it looks as though the spade queen is the last chance. Yes, that does it. Declarer needs a spade ruff and when East comes in with ♠ J he will lead a heart, breaking the squeeze.

11

West was similarly overburdened on the next deal and, like a company executive, should have attempted to delegate some of his responsibility.

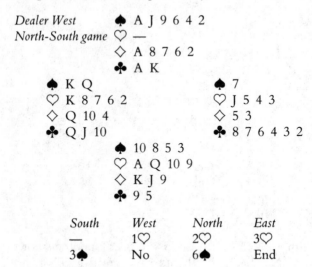

Dealer West
♠ A J 9 6 4 2
North-South game
♡ —
◇ A 8 7 6 2
♣ A K

♠ K Q
♡ K 8 7 6 2
◇ Q 10 4
♣ Q J 10

♠ 7
♡ J 5 4 3
◇ 5 3
♣ 8 7 6 4 3 2

♠ 10 8 5 3
♡ A Q 10 9
◇ K J 9
♣ 9 5

South	West	North	East
—	1♡	2♡	3♡
3♠	No	6♠	End

West led the queen of clubs, won in dummy. Spurning the safety play in spades (low from dummy on the first round), South cashed the second club and played ace and another spade, hoping for a favourable return from West.

The danger of leading either a diamond or a club was apparent and West exited with a low heart, which ran to the jack and queen. South now cashed the ace of hearts and took the ruffing finesse against West to obtain three diamond discards – on ♡ Q, ♡ A, and ♡ 9.

'We're all right if you don't put in the jack of hearts,' West observed learnedly.

Not so. Declarer can cash the ace of hearts and run dummy's remaining trumps to squeeze West in the red suits. Can you see a sure defence? West must exit with the *king* of hearts when he wins the spade. East can then assume responsibility for the hearts, West for the diamonds.

12

2

The first hurdle

Many a makeable contract is dead and buried by the time the first trick has been quitted. Surprising, since the instruction to stop and think at trick one is drummed into most bridge players when they are still in short trousers.

Perhaps the most common type of decision is whether or not to finesse at trick one. Declarer on the next deal did decide to finesse, thinking his battlements impregnable. He was soon proved wrong.

```
Dealer South        ♠ K 10 5
Love all            ♡ A J 6
                    ◇ 8 3
                    ♣ K J 10 9 2
  ♠ 8 3                             ♠ J 9 7 6 2
  ♡ 10 8 7 4 2                      ♡ K 5
  ◇ A Q 9 7                         ◇ 5 4 2
  ♣ 7 4                             ♣ A 8 6
                    ♠ A Q 4
                    ♡ Q 9 3
                    ◇ K J 10 6
                    ♣ Q 5 3
```

South	West	North	East
1NT	No	3NT	End

West led ♡ 4 and declarer nodded approvingly at dummy's assets. 'Small, please,' he said.

East won with the king and switched to a diamond,

covered by the jack and queen. Back came ◇ 9, pinning dummy's 8. Declarer had no option but to win the trick and clear the club suit. No reprieve was forthcoming. East won the trick and led a third round of diamonds. West had ◇ A 7 over South's ◇ K 6 and the contract went one down.

South should have played ♡ A at trick one. After clearing the club suit he would have eight tricks on top and a ninth would be readily available in hearts.

The correct first move is not always so obvious. Try this one from an international trial in Australia, where the bidding – like the continent – is often upside down. South somehow became the declarer in six hearts.

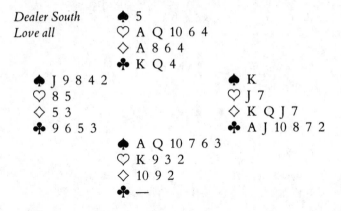

Dealer South
Love all

♠ 5
♡ A Q 10 6 4
◇ A 8 6 4
♣ K Q 4

♠ J 9 8 4 2   ♠ K
♡ 8 5   ♡ J 7
◇ 5 3   ◇ K Q J 7
♣ 9 6 5 3   ♣ A J 10 8 7 2

♠ A Q 10 7 6 3
♡ K 9 3 2
◇ 10 9 2
♣ —

East had shown clubs in the course of the bidding, and West attacked in that suit. Dummy's king was covered by the ace. What would you do now as South? Ruff and then try to form a plan of some sort?

The Australian declarer, Peter Gill, decided that there might be some advantage in discarding on this first trick. Establishing the spade suit was the most realistic plan for making the contract, and preserving his four-card trump holding would increase the prospects of achieving this. It would give the South hand an extra entry later in the play.

Declining to ruff, declarer discarded a diamond on the ace of clubs. East switched to the king of diamonds, won by dummy's ace. A spade was played to the king and ace, and declarer ruffed a spade with the queen of hearts. After drawing trumps with the ace and king, he ruffed another spade and discarded his last diamond on the queen of clubs. Two trumps were left in hand, so declarer was able to establish and enjoy the thirteenth spade. Had he ruffed at trick one, eleven tricks would have been the limit.

Sometimes the void in the suit led is faced by a winner in the dummy. You then have to decide whether to take the winner straightaway or wait until later, when more information may be to hand. On this deal declarer came to the wrong answer:

Dealer South ♠ J 9 7 4
Game all ♡ J 8 5
　　　　　　　 ◇ A 7 2
　　　　　　　 ♣ 10 6 2

♠ 10 8 3 2　　　　　　　♠ Q 5
♡ 6 4　　　　　　　　　♡ A 2
◇ Q 9 8 6　　　　　　　◇ K J 10 5 4 3
♣ Q 4 3　　　　　　　　♣ 9 8 7

　　　　　　　 ♠ A K 6
　　　　　　　 ♡ K Q 10 9 7 3
　　　　　　　 ◇ —
　　　　　　　 ♣ A K J 5

South	West	North	East
2♣	No	2◇	Dble
2♡	No	3♡	No
4♣	No	4◇	No
6♡	End		

15

North's cue bid of four diamonds was not good news to South, but he was entitled to think that the contract would depend on the club finesse, at worst.

West led a diamond against six hearts and South played the ace from dummy, discarding ♠ 6 from hand. He later brought down the queen of spades in two rounds, but the jack provided only one discard and the club finesse could not be avoided. When this failed, South was one down.

It was not easy to convince the declarer that he had thrown away the contract on the first trick. 'How could it be right to throw a club on the ace of diamonds?' he protested. 'The club finesse must be a better chance than finding East with a doubleton queen of spades.'

This was true, but two slices of salt beef are better than one, as the saying goes. South should postpone his decision by ruffing at trick one. Let's say the defenders return another diamond when they take the ace of trumps. Declarer must ruff again. After drawing trumps he cashes ♠ A K. When the queen falls he can finesse the 9 and discard one club on the jack of spades and another on the ace of diamonds.

(What did you say? East might have played the queen of spades from Q 10 x? In that case, be sure to nobble him for your team next year.)

Nothing is lost if the spade queen does not fall, of course. Declarer can revert to the original line, discarding a spade and relying on a favourable club position.

The next deal is similar at first glance; again you have an ace facing a void in the suit led. It's a double-dummy problem, though, so you can can be sure that the solution will be amusing or spectacular.

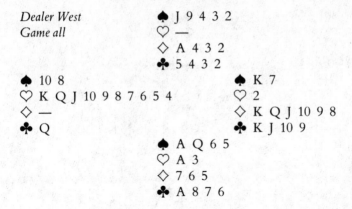

Dealer West
Game all

```
              ♠ J 9 4 3 2
              ♡ —
              ◇ A 4 3 2
              ♣ 5 4 3 2
♠ 10 8                        ♠ K 7
♡ K Q J 10 9 8 7 6 5 4        ♡ 2
◇ —                           ◇ K Q J 10 9 8
♣ Q                           ♣ K J 10 9
              ♠ A Q 6 5
              ♡ A 3
              ◇ 7 6 5
              ♣ A 8 7 6
```

There is no bidding in a double-dummy problem, but you may imagine that South opens one spade, West overcalls four hearts, and North bids four spades, perhaps doubled by East. West leads the king of hearts. How can South make ten tricks?

If you have some experience of the mentality of problem setters, you may not find it too difficult; but if you have led a sheltered life you might spend several hours without coming close to the solution.

Have you done your best? This is the answer: ruff the opening lead and dispose of the ace of hearts (obviously!), retaining ♡ 3 as an exit card. Now draw trumps, cash the ace of clubs and put West on lead with the low heart. The poor fellow in the West seat now has to lead two more hearts, on which you discard diamonds from the dummy and clubs from your own hand. West is still on lead in this end position:

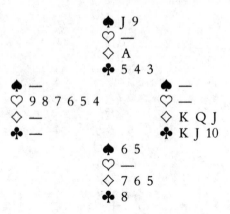

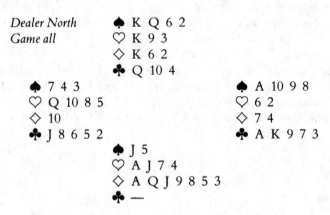

You ruff the next heart in dummy and discard your last club from hand. East is caught in a trump squeeze. You can establish a winner in whichever suit he discards.

The last few hands would be bread and butter to the sort of player who makes a study of rare endgames. He might not shine on the next hand, though, for it requires the touch of an artist. It was played by the Frenchman, Le Royer, in a match against a team from Bulgaria.

South	West	North	East
—	—	1♣	2♣
2◇	No	2NT	No
3♡	No	3♠	No
4◇	No	5◇	No
6◇	End		

East, knowing that one club might be a short suit, overcalled with a natural two clubs. This was helpful to South, since it meant that North would hold strength in the other suits.

West led ♣ 5 against six diamonds and two critical plays were made on the first trick. South played low from dummy – not the 10 – and East played the king, thinking it could hardly matter. He was soon disillusioned. Le Royer ruffed the king of clubs, drew trumps and led a spade to the king and ace. East returned a spade to the jack and South crossed to dummy with a third trump to cash the queen of spades. When the queen of clubs was led from dummy East had to cover and the club guard was transferred to the West hand. Since West had to guard the heart suit also, he was squeezed when South played off all the diamonds.

Declarer's play of ♣ 4 at trick one was an excellent shot. Putting in the 10 could gain only if West held both the king and jack, a remote prospect after East's overcall.

East had no excuse for his failure to play the 9, though. The bidding marked declarer with at most a singleton club. It couldn't be the jack because West would not have led the 5 from ♣ 8 6 5 2.

3

Unusual moves in defence

Some people, not the present authors, take great delight in buying a dilapidated property and restoring it to its pristine condition. Much more satisfying, they say, than moving straight into a brand-new house. You can see what they mean, up to a point. Success is generally more satisfying when it has been hard won.

In a bridge context the part of the game requiring the most hard work and application is undoubtedly defence. The rewards for mastering it are correspondingly worth while, though, both in terms of personal satisfaction and matchpoints. In this chapter we shall look at some of the more unusual moves at the defenders' disposal.

Try this one as a defensive problem from the West seat:

Dealer North ♠ J 9 6 5
North-South game ♡ K 8 7 3 2
  ◇ Q 9 5
  ♣ 2

♠ A
♡ J 6 5
◇ J 8 7 4 3
♣ J 8 5 3

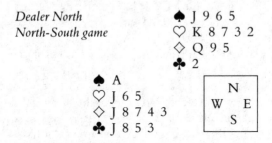

The bidding has gone:

South	West	North	East
	—	No	No
1♠	No	2♠	3♣
3♡	5♣	5♡	No
6♡	No	6♠	End

You lead a club to the queen and ace. Declarer returns the king of spades to your ace, partner following with the 4, and you must decide on your next move.

You can draw certain conclusions from the auction, particularly from the bids that were *not* made. Your partner didn't open three clubs, so he is likely to hold only six clubs. Nor did he make a Lightner double, so it is unlikely that he has a heart void. It looks as though South has five spades and that his distribution (he was willing to play in six hearts, remember) is 5–4–2–2. To advance to a slam facing a single raise he must have a fair quota of high cards, something like ♠ K Q 10 8 3 ♡ A Q 10 4 ◇ A 6 ♣ A 6. No chance to beat the contract if that's his hand, but what if his hearts are A Q 10 9? Then the heart suit would be blocked. We can more or less 'see' all four hands now:

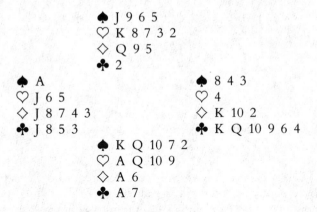

```
            ♠ J 9 6 5
            ♡ K 8 7 3 2
            ◇ Q 9 5
            ♣ 2
♠ A                      ♠ 8 4 3
♡ J 6 5                  ♡ 4
◇ J 8 7 4 3              ◇ K 10 2
♣ J 8 5 3               ♣ K Q 10 9 6 4
            ♠ K Q 10 7 2
            ♡ A Q 10 9
            ◇ A 6
            ♣ A 7
```

When in with the ace of spades you must lead a second club. This reduces the dummy to three trumps and prevents declarer scoring five heart tricks.

If South senses the heart position (quite possible when East shows up with three trumps alongside his six clubs), he may try to run ♡ 9 at some stage. You must annoy him by covering with the jack.

A final point worth noting is that the contract could have been beaten quite easily by a heart lead and a subsequent ruff. The chosen club lead was unlikely to be productive; South could hardly be missing both black aces.

The next deal is similar in that the defender could form a clear picture of all four hands when the time came to make his critical play. It is from a European Championship clash between France and Poland.

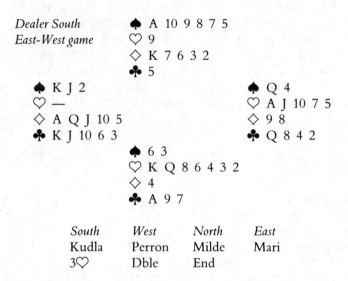

Dealer South   ♠ A 10 9 8 7 5
East-West game   ♡ 9
         ◇ K 7 6 3 2
         ♣ 5

♠ K J 2   ♠ Q 4
♡ —   ♡ A J 10 7 5
◇ A Q J 10 5   ◇ 9 8
♣ K J 10 6 3   ♣ Q 8 4 2

         ♠ 6 3
         ♡ K Q 8 6 4 3 2
         ◇ 4
         ♣ A 9 7

South	West	North	East
Kudla	Perron	Milde	Mari
3♡	Dble	End	

The play went very well for the declarer, who seems to have about six losers. West led the ace of diamonds and continued with a diamond to dummy's king, South discarding a spade. Declarer now ruffed a diamond, crossed to the ace of spades and ruffed another diamond. After the ace of clubs and a club ruff, a fifth round of diamonds was led. East ruffed with the 10 and declarer overruffed. South still held ♡ K 8 6 4 over East's ♡ A J 7 5 and could not be denied a further two tricks for his contract. (He still had an off-play card in clubs.)

What went wrong for the defence? Look at the position when dummy's fourth diamond was led:

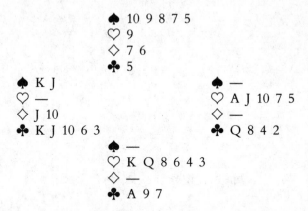

♠ 10 9 8 7 5
♡ 9
♢ 7 6
♣ 5

♠ K J
♡ —
♢ J 10
♣ K J 10 6 3

♠ —
♡ A J 10 7 5
♢ —
♣ Q 8 4 2

♠ —
♡ K Q 8 6 4 3
♢ —
♣ A 9 7

At this stage East has an accurate count of the South hand, although he may expect him to hold ♣ K x x rather than ♣ A x x. Suppose he makes the unusual play of ruffing dummy's fourth diamond with the *ace* of hearts and exiting with the jack. Now he must make two more hearts and a club, five tricks in all. It may seem unnatural to ruff high when you know that declarer will throw a loser, but the jack of hearts return robs declarer of a club ruff *and* an entry to dummy. This play would have been effective even on the third round of diamonds.

When the declarer knows exactly how the cards lie, he expects to play more or less perfectly. For some odd reason a defender who is in possession of all the facts seldom manages to play so well. West must have amazed himself by his misdefence on the next deal, from rubber bridge:

Dealer North
Game all

	♠ Q 8 6 2	
	♡ A K 3	
	◇ 9 7	
	♣ A K Q J	

♠ K 10 9 7		♠ J
♡ 8 4 2		♡ 9 7 5
◇ A Q 6 3		◇ K 10 8 4
♣ 10 6		♣ 9 8 5 4 2

	♠ A 5 4 3	
	♡ Q J 10 6	
	◇ J 5 2	
	♣ 7 3	

South	West	North	East
—	—	1♣	No
1♡	No	1♠	No
2♠	No	4♡	End

North should have bid only three hearts, forcing, at his third turn. He leapt to four hearts, however, and everyone passed. West led a trump and South drew three rounds, followed by four rounds of clubs, discarding two diamonds. He then played a spade to the ace, arriving at this position:

	♠ Q 8 6	
	♡ —	
	◇ 9 7	
	♣ —	

♠ K 10 9		♠ —
♡ —		♡ —
◇ A Q		◇ K 10 8 4
♣ —		♣ 9

	♠ 5 4 3	
	♡ J	
	◇ J	
	♣ —	

24

South led a second spade and the 10 appeared from West. After some thought declarer took the wrong view, playing low from dummy. East, sensing that the contract might now go down, played ◇ 10 with a meaning look.

He might as well not have bothered. Instead of leading the queen of diamonds, letting East overtake and play a club to force South's last trump, West busily played *ace* and another diamond. Dummy's spade queen, reprieved from her death sentence, took the thirteenth trick.

Clever plays like the Q from A Q in the last example may draw an admiring glance from the kibitzers. But good play in defence, like good acting, need not be dramatic. West's accurate play on this deal might easily pass unnoticed by the majority of the audience.

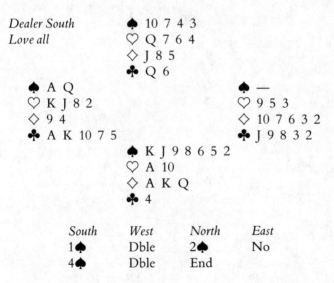

Dealer South
Love all

	♠ 10 7 4 3	
	♡ Q 7 6 4	
	◇ J 8 5	
	♣ Q 6	

♠ A Q		♠ —
♡ K J 8 2		♡ 9 5 3
◇ 9 4		◇ 10 7 6 3 2
♣ A K 10 7 5		♣ J 9 8 3 2

	♠ K J 9 8 6 5 2	
	♡ A 10	
	◇ A K Q	
	♣ 4	

South	West	North	East
1♠	Dble	2♠	No
4♠	Dble	End	

South was wise not to redouble, since this might have prompted East to bid 4 NT. Five clubs goes only one down.

West began his defence against four spades doubled with

the ace of clubs, drawing the 6, 2 and 4. It seems natural enough to continue with the king of clubs, doesn't it? See what happens if you do. Declarer will ruff and cash three diamond winners. Sooner or later you will be thrown in to lead a heart or concede a ruff-and-discard.

Partner's ♣ 2 at trick one proclaims an odd number of cards in the suit, doubtless five since declarer would scarcely have ventured to the four level with three small clubs. West should therefore put his king of clubs to one side after the first trick. Although it is not fated to score a trick, it may be invaluable as an exit card later. If West switches to a diamond at trick two declarer is held to nine tricks.

In retrospect, West's play on the last hand was not too difficult. He could see the possible endplay staring him in the face. The next deal is more difficult because partner is the one threatened with the endplay.

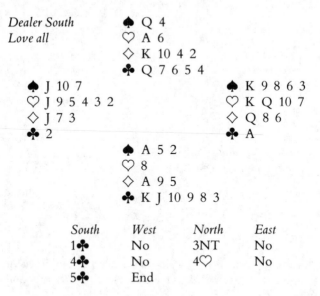

```
Dealer South        ♠ Q 4
Love all            ♡ A 6
                    ◇ K 10 4 2
                    ♣ Q 7 6 5 4
   ♠ J 10 7                        ♠ K 9 8 6 3
   ♡ J 9 5 4 3 2                   ♡ K Q 10 7
   ◇ J 7 3                         ◇ Q 8 6
   ♣ 2                             ♣ A
                    ♠ A 5 2
                    ♡ 8
                    ◇ A 9 5
                    ♣ K J 10 9 8 3
```

South	West	North	East
1♣	No	3NT	No
4♣	No	4♡	No
5♣	End		

You may not think much of North's 3 NT, but at

rubber bridge some players favour bids of this kind. South, rightly as it happens, was not confident of game in no-trumps and directed the partnership towards the club game.

West led the jack of spades and South, a shrewd operator, let him hold the trick. West continued unawares with a second spade and now there was a simple elimination. South ruffed the losers in spades and hearts, then played a trump to East's ace. East tried to squirm off the hook by leading the queen of diamonds, but declarer was ready for this. He won with the ace and finessed against West's jack.

'I did my best, partner,' observed East, quite pleased with his queen of diamonds play.

North congratulated South on his view in diamonds, but nobody noticed the most interesting feature of the deal. Not obvious, but West does better to switch to a trump at trick two. East then has a safe exit in either major and the defenders must come to a diamond trick.

The next hand starts in the same way. You win the first trick and have to make the key play at trick two. If you feel in the mood, cover the East and South hands and treat it as a defensive problem.

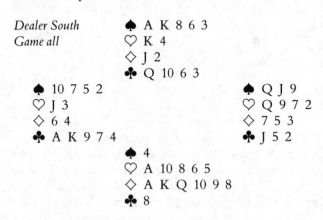

Dealer South
Game all

North
♠ A K 8 6 3
♡ K 4
♢ J 2
♣ Q 10 6 3

West
♠ 10 7 5 2
♡ J 3
♢ 6 4
♣ A K 9 7 4

East
♠ Q J 9
♡ Q 9 7 2
♢ 7 5 3
♣ J 5 2

South
♠ 4
♡ A 10 8 6 5
♢ A K Q 10 9 8
♣ 8

South	West	North	East
1◇	No	1♠	No
2♡	No	3♣[1]	No
3♡	No	4◇	No
5♣	No	6◇	End

[1] After partner's reverse North is too good for a probably terminal 3 NT.

You cash the ace of clubs, drawing the 3, 2 and 8. It seems from the bidding that declarer's shape is 1–5–6–1. What is the best move at trick 2?

A heart would clearly be pointless, and at the table West switched to ◇ 4, hoping to reduce declarer's heart ruffs. South took one heart ruff, then played off his trumps, arriving at this ending:

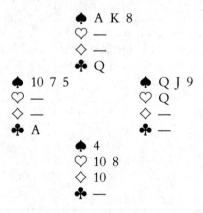

```
                    ♠ A K 8
                    ♡ —
                    ◇ —
                    ♣ Q
     ♠ 10 7 5                    ♠ Q J 9
     ♡ —                         ♡ Q
     ◇ —                         ◇ —
     ♣ A                         ♣ —
                    ♠ 4
                    ♡ 10 8
                    ◇ 10
                    ♣ —
```

Declarer's last trump exerted a typical double squeeze, each defender in turn having to discard a spade. West could have prevented this with a little more thought at trick 2. His switch to ◇ 4 was a mirage. If South set out to ruff hearts, the ◇ 4 would force the jack and declarer would not be able to ruff twice anyhow. A stronger but less obvious defence was available. West should switch to a spade, destroying the communication card for a squeeze.

The defenders missed an early chance on the next hand, too, but they had an opportunity to redeem themselves in the endgame.

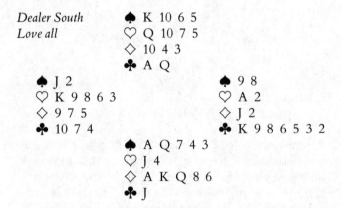

Dealer South
Love all

North
♠ K 10 6 5
♡ Q 10 7 5
◇ 10 4 3
♣ A Q

West
♠ J 2
♡ K 9 8 6 3
◇ 9 7 5
♣ 10 7 4

East
♠ 9 8
♡ A 2
◇ J 2
♣ K 9 8 6 5 3 2

South
♠ A Q 7 4 3
♡ J 4
◇ A K Q 8 6
♣ J

South opened one spade and North raised to three spades. There is much to be said for a direct six spades on the South hand, but modern tournament players are nervous of such adventures and South bid four diamonds. North now bid five clubs and East gave this a moment's thought before passing. Thinking now that West might lead a club against six spades (it sounds as if he would have done so himself), South bid the slam.

However, West was aware that his partner's hesitation had been noted and was afraid that the opposition might claim a foul if he led a club. Instead he tried a diamond. After five rounds of spades and four diamonds, South reached this position:

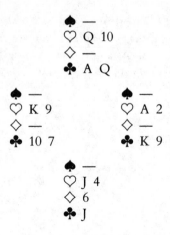

```
              ♠ —
              ♡ Q 10
              ♢ —
              ♣ A Q
  ♠ —                        ♠ —
  ♡ K 9                      ♡ A 2
  ♢ —                        ♢ —
  ♣ 10 7                     ♣ K 9
              ♠ —
              ♡ J 4
              ♢ 6
              ♣ J
```

On the last diamond West threw a club, which no doubt seemed natural. A heart was thrown from dummy and East was in trouble. He was bound to be endplayed if he threw a low heart, so he finally chose the ace of hearts. South crossed to the ace of clubs and led the queen of hearts, winkling the last trick with his jack of hearts.

Look back at the end position. West had no need to keep a guard to his heart king; declarer has twelve tricks if he holds the ace. It's strange, but a discard of ♡ 9 beats the contract. If dummy throws a heart East parts with the ace of hearts, and if dummy throws a club, so does East.

Sometimes in defence you have no alternative but to unguard an honour in one of declarer's suits. Provided you can do this with the air of a man on a Sunday stroll, there is no reason why declarer should diagnose the situation. As with other deceptions, though, your partner may have an important supporting role to play. Look at this deal:

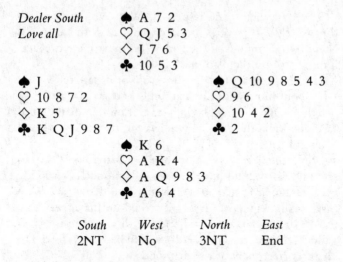

Dealer South   ♠ A 7 2
Love all   ♡ Q J 5 3
           ♢ J 7 6
           ♣ 10 5 3

♠ J   ♠ Q 10 9 8 5 4 3
♡ 10 8 7 2   ♡ 9 6
♢ K 5   ♢ 10 4 2
♣ K Q J 9 8 7   ♣ 2

           ♠ K 6
           ♡ A K 4
           ♢ A Q 9 8 3
           ♣ A 6 4

South	*West*	*North*	*East*
2NT	No	3NT	End

West leads the king of clubs, which is allowed to hold. East shows out on the next round and declarer wins with the ace. He has nothing better to do at the moment than play four rounds of hearts. Surprisingly West follows all the way, East discarding two spades. Declarer now cashes the spade king to leave this position:

           ♠ A 7
           ♡ —
           ♢ J 7 6
           ♣ 10

♠ —   ♠ Q 10 9
♡ —   ♡ —
♢ K 5   ♢ 10 4 2
♣ J 9 8 7   ♣ —

           ♠ 6
           ♡ —
           ♢ A Q 9 8
           ♣ 6

When another spade is played, West cannot afford to throw a club. If he does, declarer will exit with a club and claim two diamonds at the end. West must therefore steel himself to bare the diamond king.

Will the contract now go down? Not if declarer has his wits about him. With the diamonds known by now to be 1–3, he cannot lose by playing ace and another diamond. If East does hold the king he will have to surrender a second diamond trick at the end.

Could the defenders have done any better? Not easy to see, but East should have thrown a diamond earlier in the play, retaining four spades and only two diamonds. With three spade winners at large, it would not have been safe for declarer to play ace and another diamond in the end-game. To make the contract he would have been forced to take a correct view of the diamond suit.

The last few hands have been hard work and we shall end the chapter on a lighter note, looking at a couple of lead-directing gadgets that can give the defenders a flying start.

The first one occurs when the opponents have used a 'splinter bid' – a jump in a new suit that shows good trump support for partner and a shortage in the suit bid. Imagine South opens one spade and North responds four clubs (showing a good raise to four spades and a control in clubs). You are sitting East with:

♠ 10 7 3
♡ 9 3 2
♢ Q 9 2
♣ A K J 3

You double to suggest a club lead? It won't help your cause very much, with at most a singleton club in dummy.

But what if the bidding had started 1 ♠ – No – 4 ♢, and you held the same hand? Now a club lead might be priceless. The Mexican expert, Dr George Rosenkranz, has suggested that a double of a splinter bid should ask for the lead of the suit *below* the splinter. The gadget would have worked well on this hand:

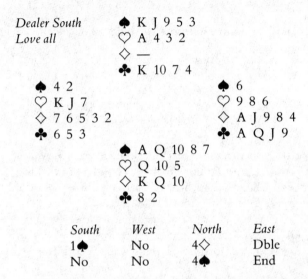

Dealer South
Love all

♠ K J 9 5 3
♡ A 4 3 2
◇ —
♣ K 10 7 4

♠ 4 2
♡ K J 7
◇ 7 6 5 3 2
♣ 6 5 3

♠ 6
♡ 9 8 6
◇ A J 9 8 4
♣ A Q J 9

♠ A Q 10 8 7
♡ Q 10 5
◇ K Q 10
♣ 8 2

South	West	North	East
1♠	No	4◇	Dble
No	No	4♠	End

East, playing normal methods, made a pointless double to show his diamonds. West duly led a diamond, and declarer made the contract by discarding a heart from dummy at trick one. He eventually discarded all dummy's heart losers on his three diamonds, losing just two clubs and a diamond.

If the defenders had been using the double according to Rosenkranz's scheme, the contract would have been defeated in quick time. A club lead followed by a heart switch would be deadly.

Another type of lead-directing double, the Lightner slam double, is played almost universally. It can be effective against game contracts as well. See if you can find the best lead on this hand, held by West in a Cavendish Invitation Pairs:

♠ 7 5
♡ K J 10 5
◇ J 4 2
♣ 8 6 5 3

Both sides are vulnerable and the bidding has been:

South	West	North	East
1♣	No	1◇	1♡
1♠	2♡	3♠	No
4♠	No	No	Dble
End			

What do you make of partner's double? He can't have much in the trump suit; nor can he be confident of making any tricks in hearts, which have been supported. So the double must ask for an abnormal lead.

Manfield, West at one table, decided to lead ♣ 8. He chose his highest club to indicate that his entry was in hearts rather than in diamonds. This was the full deal:

```
              ♠ J 6 3 2
              ♡ 6 2
              ◇ K Q 5
              ♣ A 9 7 2
  ♠ 7 5                      ♠ 10 9 4
  ♡ K J 10 5                 ♡ A 8 7 4 3
  ◇ J 4 2                    ◇ A 10 9 8 7
  ♣ 8 6 5 3                  ♣ —
              ♠ A K Q 8
              ♡ Q 9
              ◇ 6 3
              ♣ K Q J 10 4
```

Woolsey, sitting East, ruffed the club lead and returned a low heart to the queen and king. After another club ruff he took his two aces, rather than try for a third ruff. He judged, rightly, that +500 would produce an excellent score. This result helped them to win the event, which carries the biggest cash prize in bridge.

Events at another table provided an ironical comparison. The bidding was the same, including the final double, but here Judy Radin led the *king* of hearts, expecting to hold the trick and decide on her next action after seeing the dummy. When her partner dropped the 3, she switched to a club. East ruffed and, instead of cashing her red aces to ensure one down, returned a *low* heart. A surprised declarer won with the queen and so made four spades doubled.

4

Keeping cool in the hot seat

The bridge community does contain a few shrinking violets who like to avoid the limelight, but don't expect to find any experts among them. Top players like to have the good cards their way, particularly in a pairs. One area of dummy play in which they reckon they have a special edge is in their ability to judge finessing situations. What may be a 50–50 guess for ordinary mortals is rarely so for the great stars of the game. Look at this effort by the Italian, De Falco, in a European championship.

Dealer South
Love all

```
                    ♠ A K J
                    ♡ Q 6 3
                    ◇ K J 8 4
                    ♣ K 3 2
  ♠ 8                                 ♠ 7 2
  ♡ A K J 9 7 5                       ♡ 8 4 2
  ◇ A 6 2                             ◇ Q 7 5 3
  ♣ A 5 4                             ♣ J 10 8 6
                    ♠ Q 10 9 6 5 4 3
                    ♡ 10
                    ◇ 10 9
                    ♣ Q 9 7
```

South	West	North	East
3♠	Dble	4♠	No
No	Dble	End	

West led the king of hearts and switched to a trump. Two lines of play might seem attractive. You could play

West for the diamond A Q, establishing a discard for your club loser, or you could play him for A x in clubs.

Falco took neither of these lines. He drew trumps with the ace and queen and led a diamond to the *king*. He then returned a diamond to the 10 and ace, leaving West on play. West was faced with three different ways of presenting declarer with a tenth trick. Had East gone in with ◇ Q, West's ace would have been ruffed down.

In the closed room the Norwegian declarer, Nordby, ended in four spades undoubled and followed exactly the same line. Quite a feast for the onlookers, as the journalists say!

Declarer on the next deal was in such a poor contract that he was forced to take the right view of the key suit. Cover the East and West hands and see if you would have got it right. The contract is seven spades and the king of hearts is led.

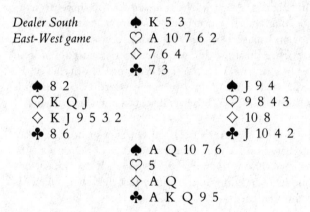

Dealer South
East-West game

♠ K 5 3
♡ A 10 7 6 2
◇ 7 6 4
♣ 7 3

♠ 8 2　　　　　　　　♠ J 9 4
♡ K Q J　　　　　　　♡ 9 8 4 3
◇ K J 9 5 3 2　　　　◇ 10 8
♣ 8 6　　　　　　　　♣ J 10 4 2

♠ A Q 10 7 6
♡ 5
◇ A Q
♣ A K Q 9 5

South	West	North	East
1♣	1◇	1♡	No
2♠	No	3♠	No
4NT	No	5◇	No
6◇[1]	No	7♠[2]	End

[1] A grand slam try.

[2] North, despite holding only three trumps, judged that his king of spades was sufficient reason for accepting.

West led the king of hearts, won by dummy's ace, and prospects looked bleak for declarer. It was quite possible that West controlled both red suits, but there were insufficient entries for a heart–diamond squeeze. Nor would it help declarer to find West with K Q J alone in hearts.

West's vulnerable overcall made it a near certainty that the diamond king was offside, so declarer went boldly for another chance. At trick 2 he finessed ♣ 9! When this hair-raising manoeuvre succeeded, he drew two rounds of trumps and played off his top clubs, discarding two diamonds from dummy. He was then able to ruff a diamond for his twelfth trick. Declarer played for the only lie of the club suit that would allow him to discard two diamonds from dummy. A 3–3 club break would have been no use to him.

More often, declarer's decision whether or not to finesse will be based on a count, or partial count, of the opponents' hands. South on the next deal managed to outwit his opponents by relying on the trusty fact that every player is dealt thirteen cards.

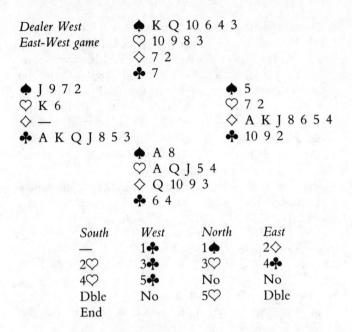

Dealer West
East-West game

	♠ K Q 10 6 4 3	
	♡ 10 9 8 3	
	◇ 7 2	
	♣ 7	

♠ J 9 7 2		♠ 5
♡ K 6		♡ 7 2
◇ —		◇ A K J 8 6 5 4
♣ A K Q J 8 5 3		♣ 10 9 2

	♠ A 8	
	♡ A Q J 5 4	
	◇ Q 10 9 3	
	♣ 6 4	

South	West	North	East
—	1♣	1♠	2◇
2♡	3♣	3♡	4♣
4♡	5♣	No	No
Dble	No	5♡	Dble
End			

West led the ace of clubs, his partner signalling with the 2, and continued with the king, which was ruffed in dummy. A trump finesse lost to the king and West returned a trump. Declarer now cashed the ace of spades and led another spade, finessing dummy's 10. He was then able to discard all his diamonds on dummy's spade suit and claim the contract. Had he not finessed ♠ 10, he would have been one down. He could have established the spades and returned to dummy with a trump, but he would be able to discard only three diamonds.

It was an annoying hand for the defenders, who had four top tricks, but couldn't arrive at them after the opening lead.

'You might have underled your clubs,' East suggested to his partner. This was somewhat unreasonable, since West had a trump trick and in any case had no reason to think that desperate measures were needed.

Why did South finesse ♠ 10 on the second round? It was not difficult really, if you remember the bidding. West was known to hold two hearts and the club distribution, in view of West's three-club call and East's signal of the 2 at trick one, was likely to be 7–3. As for the diamonds, West had had two opportunities to lead the suit bid by his partner, but had spurned both. He had to be void, and this marked him with 4–2–0–7 distribution. Declarer's play on this deal illustrated the two main ingredients of expert play: deduction and counting.

The next deal is similar in a way, although the Italian star Arturo Franco in fact misguessed the crucial suit. Let's inspect the evidence and see if he might have got it right.

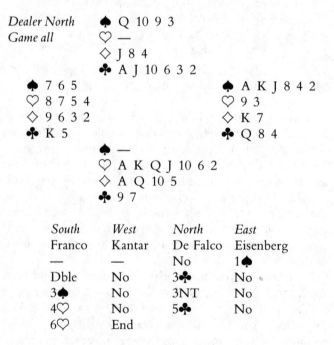

Dealer North
Game all

♠ Q 10 9 3
♡ —
◇ J 8 4
♣ A J 10 6 3 2

♠ 7 6 5
♡ 8 7 5 4
◇ 9 6 3 2
♣ K 5

♠ A K J 8 4 2
♡ 9 3
◇ K 7
♣ Q 8 4

♠ —
♡ A K Q J 10 6 2
◇ A Q 10 5
♣ 9 7

South	West	North	East
Franco	Kantar	De Falco	Eisenberg
—	—	No	1♠
Dble	No	3♣	No
3♠	No	3NT	No
4♡	No	5♣	No
6♡	End		

After a spirited auction West led ♠ 5, following the

modern style of low from three small. Declarer ruffed and drew trumps in four rounds. He then led a low club, on which Kantar smartly played the king, the standard entry-killer.

Franco won with the ace and used his only entry to dummy to lead the jack of diamonds. East covered and declarer eventually lost a diamond trick to West.

It would have been slightly better play for declarer to duck the first round of clubs (for one thing, the queen of clubs might then fall under the ace). West's best exit would be another club, won by dummy's ace. Declarer would then have a fair amount of information. He knows the heart position and may well take the view that East holds the outstanding ♣ Q. As for the spades, surely they are 3–6. If West held four spades and the king of clubs he would have bid two spades over South's double. This gives East a 6–2–2–3 shape and the winning play, after taking the ace of clubs, is a *low* diamond from dummy, not the jack.

Enough of finesses. Let's look at another important technique – that of establishing a side suit in dummy. Some of the plays involved are so baffling that even with all the cards exposed the winning play is not apparent – unless you have dwelt in those areas before.

Suppose you arrive in six spades on the deal overleaf and a trump is led. How would you set about it? (Cover the East–West hands if you're feeling industrious.)

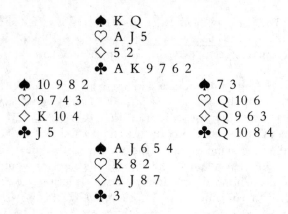

♠ K Q
♡ A J 5
♢ 5 2
♣ A K 9 7 6 2

♠ 10 9 8 2   ♠ 7 3
♡ 9 7 4 3   ♡ Q 10 6
♢ K 10 4   ♢ Q 9 6 3
♣ J 5   ♣ Q 10 8 4

♠ A J 6 5 4
♡ K 8 2
♢ A J 8 7
♣ 3

With a hand not easy to express, North bid simply two clubs over South's one spade. The bidding continued:

South	West	North	East
1♠	No	2♣	No
2♢	No	2♡	No
2NT	No	3♠	No
4♠	No	6♠	End

West leads ♠ 10 and if you haven't seen this type of hand before the likelihood is that you will start on the clubs, playing the ace and ruffing the second round. You play another spade to dummy and lead another low club, but this time you are overruffed. The clubs are established now, but you are a trick short. You make only four spades in hand (one was overruffed), four clubs and three red winners.

Now try again. Having won the spade lead in dummy, lead a *low* club at trick 2. The defence can do nothing to overcome this exotic play. Say that East wins and returns a diamond. You win, draw a second trump and ruff a low club. Now you extract the remaining trumps and have four club winners on the table.

The play would be interesting on a heart lead to the

king. If you aim to follow a similar line, ducking the first round of clubs to East (who cannot remove the heart entry), West can thwart you by inserting the jack.

Here is a similar hand that is said to have defeated all the competitors at a tournament in Cannes.

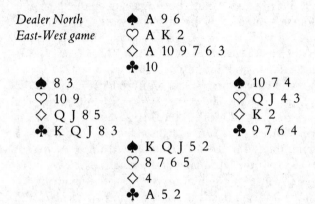

Dealer North
East-West game

♠ A 9 6
♡ A K 2
◇ A 10 9 7 6 3
♣ 10

♠ 8 3
♡ 10 9
◇ Q J 8 5
♣ K Q J 8 3

♠ 10 7 4
♡ Q J 4 3
◇ K 2
♣ 9 7 6 4

♠ K Q J 5 2
♡ 8 7 6 5
◇ 4
♣ A 5 2

South plays in six spades and captures West's club lead with the ace. At this point the normal sequence went like this: ace of diamonds, diamond ruff, club ruff, diamond ruff, ace of trumps. The lead is in dummy and these cards are left:

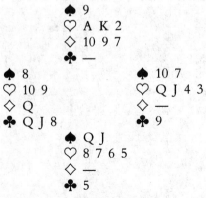

♠ 9
♡ A K 2
◇ 10 9 7
♣ —

♠ 8
♡ 10 9
◇ Q
♣ Q J 8

♠ 10 7
♡ Q J 4 3
◇ —
♣ 9

♠ Q J
♡ 8 7 6 5
◇ —
♣ 5

43

Declarer's only chance now is to concede a diamond trick to West, discarding a club or a heart from hand. He goes one down, though. He cannot survive a club return from West.

A commentator at the time suggested a different, and better, line in which South discards a club on the third, not the fourth, round of diamonds. This works well enough. West exits with a heart, say, and another diamond establishes the suit. Declarer draws trumps, discarding a heart from the table, and dummy is high.

This sequence would be less comfortable if East held the long clubs, though. The best play (if you are not trying for an overtrick) is to duck the very first diamond. When West returns a heart you ruff a diamond, ruff a club, ruff a diamond (high if necessary), then draw trumps. As on the previous deal, the advantage of ducking the first round is that you reduce to a minimum the risk of an overruff.

On the last two hands declarer had to take a ruff at the right time. On the next hand his aim is to stop the defenders taking a ruff at the *wrong* time.

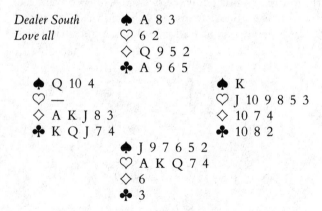

Dealer South ♠ A 8 3
Love all   ♡ 6 2
      ♢ Q 9 5 2
      ♣ A 9 6 5

♠ Q 10 4   ♠ K
♡ —   ♡ J 10 9 8 5 3
♢ A K J 8 3   ♢ 10 7 4
♣ K Q J 7 4   ♣ 10 8 2

      ♠ J 9 7 6 5 2
      ♡ A K Q 7 4
      ♢ 6
      ♣ 3

South	West	North	East
1♠	2NT	Dble	No
3♡	No	3♠	No
4♠	End		

West cashed the ace of diamonds and switched to the king of clubs, won by dummy's ace. The question now is – which card should declarer play next?

The original declarer didn't take long to make his choice. 'Ace of trumps, please,' he said.

The contract could no longer be made. At the next trick West ruffed the ace of hearts and cashed the master queen of trumps. Declarer was a trick short.

Certainly it was unlucky to find West with three trumps, but it is possible to cater for this distribution. If West does have three trumps his shape is probably 3–0–5–5. See what happens if declarer plays a heart to the ace at trick 3. West can ruff and return a trump (as good as anything), but the contract is impregnable. Declarer wins the trump switch with the ace and plays another high heart, eventually losing just two trumps and a diamond. Had West followed to the ace of hearts, there would not be room for him to hold three trumps. It would then be safe to play the ace of trumps.

Even better, possibly, than a heart to the ace at trick 3 is to begin with a club ruff, followed by ♡ A, spade to the ace, club ruff. This would give you chances of a trump coup if East held all four spades.

West's 2NT intervention was a fair proposition on the previous hand (he had two good suits), but more often than not the convention is misused. When the suits are poor and there is little chance of buying the contract, this is the sort of result to expect:

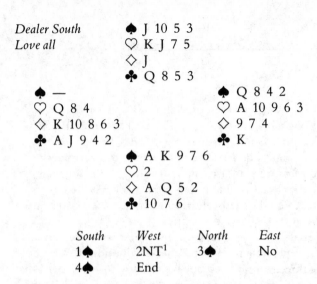

Dealer South
Love all

♠ J 10 5 3
♡ K J 7 5
♢ J
♣ Q 8 5 3

♠ —
♡ Q 8 4
♢ K 10 8 6 3
♣ A J 9 4 2

♠ Q 8 4 2
♡ A 10 9 6 3
♢ 9 7 4
♣ K

♠ A K 9 7 6
♡ 2
♢ A Q 5 2
♣ 10 7 6

South	West	North	East
1♠	2NT[1]	3♠	No
4♠	End		

[1] Typical of the breed. The only effect is to assist the opponents in both bidding and play.

West led a low heart, covered by the jack and ace. East cashed the king of clubs and returned a diamond, won by the ace. Declarer ruffed a diamond with ♠ J and cashed the heart king, discarding his third diamond.

It was clear now that West, who was marked with ♡ Q x x, had 0–3–5–5 distribution. Having reached this conclusion, South finessed ♠ 7 on the first round and ruffed his last diamond with ♠ 10. These cards remained:

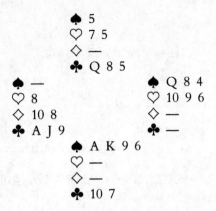

```
              ♠ 5
              ♡ 7 5
              ◇ —
              ♣ Q 8 5
♠ —                        ♠ Q 8 4
♡ 8                        ♡ 10 9 6
◇ 10 8                     ◇ —
♣ A J 9                    ♣ —
              ♠ A K 9 6
              ♡ —
              ◇ —
              ♣ 10 7
```

Thanks to the foresight in ruffing two diamonds high, declarer could now lead ♠ 5 to his 9 and draw the remaining trumps. One trick was still to come from dummy's queen of clubs, so the game was made. Well played, certainly, but quite impossible without the aid of West's revealing 2NT.

Can you see any defence after the first two tricks (heart to the ace, ♣ K)? Well, try the queen of spades at trick 3! Then, after diamond ruff, spade to hand, diamond ruff, South must shorten himself with a heart ruff and can no longer make a trick in clubs.

5

Imaginative deception

For many players bridge is a game of one-upmanship. They are driven, not by the prospect of winning master-points or magnums of Scotch whisky, but by the desire to prove themselves superior to their fellow competitors. That is where the satisfaction lies.

Gaining tricks by deception is regarded by many as the summit of one-upmanship. Many of the keenest minds in bridge have studied this area, and a great number of attractive manoeuvres have already come to light. Still, we think in this chapter you will encounter a few surprises.

Look at the first deal for a while, imagining that South plays in 3NT and West leads a spade.

Dealer South
East–West game

	♠ A 5	
	♡ 8 6 3	
	♢ A Q J 9 3	
	♣ 9 4 2	
♠ J 10 9 6 4 3		♠ Q 8 2
♡ J		♡ Q 10 9 7 5 2
♢ 7 5		♢ K 10 8
♣ K J 10 6		♣ 7
	♠ K 7	
	♡ A K 4	
	♢ 6 4 2	
	♣ A Q 8 5 3	

South	West	North	East
1♣	No	1♢	No
1NT	No	3NT	End

Declarer wins the jack of spades in hand. The diamond suit offers good prospects of four tricks, but South, seeking an additional chance, may start by cashing the ace of clubs. If West has the wit to contribute the king to this trick, declarer will doubtless place East with ♣ J 10 x x and continue with a low club to the 9. Swift disillusionment will follow when West pounces with the 10 and clears the spade suit.

If declarer is deviously minded himself, he may take a second look at West's king of clubs. If he suspects it is a false card, he has a counter. He can cross to the diamond *ace* and lead a club from dummy. When East shows out, it is not too late to put on the queen of clubs and switch back to diamonds.

West's play of the king of clubs was, admittedly, a difficult one to find. Such plays become possible only if you put yourself into the mind of the opponent. Why is he cashing the ace of clubs, you must ask yourself.

Similarly, you may wonder why a good player sometimes dabbles in all the side suits instead of drawing trumps first, as you were taught in your youth. The reason may be that he is trying to build a picture of the distribution that will tell him how to play the trump suit.

The defenders can join in that game, too. On this deal North–South would have stayed short of game but for a push from West.

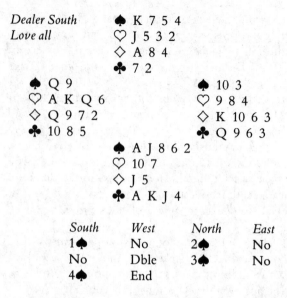

Dealer South
Love all

♠ K 7 5 4
♡ J 5 3 2
♢ A 8 4
♣ 7 2

♠ Q 9
♡ A K Q 6
♢ Q 9 7 2
♣ 10 8 5

♠ 10 3
♡ 9 8 4
♢ K 10 6 3
♣ Q 9 6 3

♠ A J 8 6 2
♡ 10 7
♢ J 5
♣ A K J 4

South	West	North	East
1♠	No	2♠	No
No	Dble	3♠	No
4♠	End		

South was close to a game try in the first place. When West reopened with a double and North advanced to three spades, South decided to bid a fourth. He reckoned that any honours partner might hold in the red suits were likely to be well placed, also that West's double would help him place the cards. In any event, it is always enjoyable to bid game after the opponents have reopened.

West began with two top hearts, then switched to a diamond, ducked to East's king. Back came ♣ 3, won by declarer's ace.

Instead of taking an early view about the trump distribution, South took a diamond ruff, cashed the king of spades and returned to the king of clubs. The position was now:

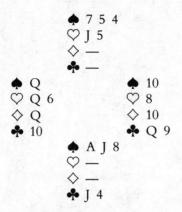

♠ 7 5 4
♡ J 5
♢ —
♣ —

♠ Q   ♠ 10
♡ Q 6   ♡ 8
♢ Q   ♢ 10
♣ 10   ♣ Q 9

♠ A J 8
♡ —
♢ —
♣ J 4

When South, still on his tour of inspection, ruffed a low
club, East followed smartly with the queen. Falling victim
to his own machinations, South placed West with 1–4–4–4
distribution and finessed the jack of spades.

As well as disguising your distribution, you will often
have chances to mislead the declarer concerning the where-
abouts of missing high cards. Imagine you are West on this
layout:

             ♢ 8 5 3

♢ A 9 4

            ♢ K played

Declarer leads ♢ 3 and plays the king from hand. Do
you take the ace? There are many situations where it will
pay you to hold off. If declarer started with K Q x he may
waste an entry to dummy to lead towards his queen. It is
also possible that declarer has K Q 10. Keep your ace
under wraps for a while and he may misguess on the next
round. (Incidentally, it is better play for the declarer –
against strong opponents – to play the *queen* from such as
K Q 10 x.)

West made a very productive hold-up on this next deal,
which was played in a pairs.

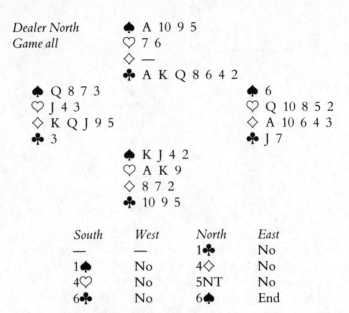

Dealer North　　　　♠ A 10 9 5
Game all　　　　　♡ 7 6
　　　　　　　　　　◇ —
　　　　　　　　　　♣ A K Q 8 6 4 2

♠ Q 8 7 3　　　　　　　　　　　♠ 6
♡ J 4 3　　　　　　　　　　　　♡ Q 10 8 5 2
◇ K Q J 9 5　　　　　　　　　◇ A 10 6 4 3
♣ 3　　　　　　　　　　　　　　♣ J 7

　　　　　　　　　　♠ K J 4 2
　　　　　　　　　　♡ A K 9
　　　　　　　　　　◇ 8 7 2
　　　　　　　　　　♣ 10 9 5

South	West	North	East
—	—	1♣	No
1♠	No	4◇	No
4♡	No	5NT	No
6♣	No	6♠	End

North's four-diamond call signified good spade support and a first-round diamond control. 5NT was trump-asking and South's response showed one of the top three honours. Against six spades West led the king of diamonds, ruffed in the dummy. When ♠ 10 was run, West followed impassively with a low card. Declarer could now see his way to thirteen tricks and an excellent pairs score. He cashed the ace of spades, blinked when East discarded, and found that he could no longer make the contract. He tried cashing the ace and king of clubs, but West had no intention of ruffing too soon – he discarded a heart. Declarer now had to cut his losses. He crossed to the ace of hearts and took a diamond ruff, eventually going two down.

The situation would have been the same if declarer had cashed the ace of trumps at trick two, followed by the 10. In fact it would have been easier for West to see that he had to hold off.

On hands of this type it is essential to retain the top cards in the trump suit. Declarer was right to run ♠ 10 at trick two, but he should have continued with ♠ 9 at the next trick. West would win this time, but it would be his last trick.

Declarer had to cope with a bad spade break on the next deal, too. It was played in a team-of-four game in two different grand slams. Both contracts had their points of interest.

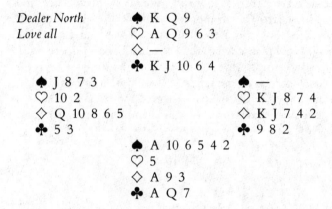

Dealer North
Love all

	♠ K Q 9	
	♡ A Q 9 6 3	
	♢ —	
	♣ K J 10 6 4	
♠ J 8 7 3		♠ —
♡ 10 2		♡ K J 8 7 4
♢ Q 10 8 6 5		♢ K J 7 4 2
♣ 5 3		♣ 9 8 2
	♠ A 10 6 5 4 2	
	♡ 5	
	♢ A 9 3	
	♣ A Q 7	

At the first table North–South did well to reach 7 NT, an excellent contract. West, with no particular malevolent intent, led ♣ 5.

Doing what comes naturally, declarer played low from dummy and captured East's 8 with the ace. A spade to dummy's king exposed the position in that suit.

It seemed to declarer that he would now need two further entries to hand – one to finesse in spades and one to enjoy the remainder of the spade suit. The only possibility was to finesse ♣ 7. Unfortunately, by the time he had worked this out, East was alive to the situation, too. When ♣ 6 was led from the table, East put in the 9. The contract was now in ruins.

South could have avoided this humiliating outcome by playing ♣ 10 at trick one, preserving two entries to hand. Naturally he expected to pay heavily for this piece of carelessness. As it turned out, he was rescued by a smart piece of deception from one of his team-mates.

In the other room the contract was seven spades – as invincible a contract as 7 NT, it would seem. West led a diamond and declarer correctly discarded a heart from the dummy. After a spade to the king declarer once again needed two entries to hand. When he played ace and another heart, East dropped the king on the second round. Declarer took the marked finesse of ♠ 9 and cashed the king. Now he needed to return to hand once more to draw the last trump. After East's play of the king of hearts it looked as though the safe play would be a third round of hearts. West's jack of spades scored the setting trick.

The next deal, from a world championship match, also provided exciting play at both tables.

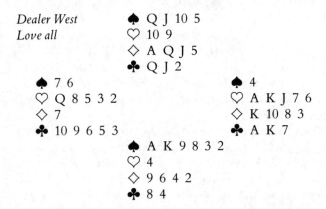

Dealer West
Love all

	♠ Q J 10 5	
	♡ 10 9	
	◇ A Q J 5	
	♣ Q J 2	
♠ 7 6		♠ 4
♡ Q 8 5 3 2		♡ A K J 7 6
◇ 7		◇ K 10 8 3
♣ 10 9 6 5 3		♣ A K 7
	♠ A K 9 8 3 2	
	♡ 4	
	◇ 9 6 4 2	
	♣ 8 4	

In the closed room Italy was East–West, USA North–South.

South	West	North	East
Eisenberg	Franco	Hamilton	Garozzo
—	No	1♢	2♡
2♠	4♡	No[1]	No
4♣	5♡	5♠[2]	Dble
End			

[1] Hoping, no doubt, that partner would double four hearts and that he would be able to express his hand well by taking out into four spades.

[2] But now he finds himself trapped, not having shown his spade support.

A diamond was led and Eisenberg managed to save a trick in the play. He won with dummy's ace, drew trumps, and played a heart from the dummy. East won with the ace, played a second top heart, and was subsequently endplayed by a club to the queen and king. 300 to East–West.

If East had let the heart run, playing his partner for the queen, declarer might still have arrived at nine tricks, but only by very precise play. He did well to lead the heart from dummy, rather than from hand.

In the other room East–West bought the contract:

South	West	North	East
Forquet	Soloway	Belladonna	Rubin
—	No	1♢	1♡
1♠	3♡	3♠	4♡
4♠	No	No	5♡
No	No	Dble	End

The defence began with two rounds of spades, East ruffing. After the ace and queen of hearts declarer led a diamond from the dummy. Belladonna won with the ace and led ♣ 2, a characteristic thrust. He had realized, no doubt, that if declarer were left to play clubs himself he might lead the 10 from dummy and take a deep finesse, pinning South's 8 if he held that card.

After long thought Rubin decided to play North for ♣ Q 8 4 2 or ♣ J 8 4 2. He rose with the ace and lost his contract. Should Rubin have fallen for this? Not really. If South did hold a singleton club honour, his shape would be 7–1–4–1 or 6–1–5–1. Holding such a massive double fit with partner he would certainly have pressed on to five spades.

After a fairly long auction, such as that above, it is usually possible to form an accurate picture of the opposing hands. The same is true when you open with a closely defined call, perhaps 1 NT or a weak two-bid, and end on the defending side. You are at an immediate disadvantage and may have to camouflage your holding to prevent declarer from reading the cards too well. This was such a hand:

Dealer East
North–South game

```
                    ♠ A K 8 6 4 2
                    ♡ A 10 5
                    ◇ 10 3
                    ♣ 9 4
♠ 7 3                              ♠ 9
♡ —                               ♡ K Q J 9 7 3
◇ Q 8 7 4 2                       ◇ 9 6 5
♣ 10 7 6 5 3 2                    ♣ K J 8
                    ♠ Q J 10 5
                    ♡ 8 6 4 2
                    ◇ A K J
                    ♣ A Q
```

South	West	North	East
—	—	—	2♡
Dble	No	3♡	No
3♠	No	5♠	No
6♠	End		

North's choice of sequence was fortunate (or well judged) in that it left South as declarer. The slam cannot be made from the North seat after a heart lead and ruff.

Against the spade slam by South, West led ♣ 5. East played the king and South won. Deciding that East had already shown his ration for a weak two-bid, and that West must hold the diamond queen, declarer played for a loser-on-loser elimination. He drew trumps, then cashed his minor suit winners and the ace of hearts, arriving at this end position:

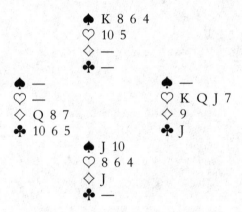

South exited in diamonds, discarding a heart from dummy, and West then had to concede a ruff-and-discard.

Do you see any way in which East might have deflected declarer from this line? When a defender who holds K J in third position can be certain that partner has not underled the ace, it is usually good play to put in the jack. For one thing, he will discover who holds the queen. Here the play may gain in a different way. If East plays the jack of clubs at trick one South may place West with the king of clubs and East with the queen of diamonds. If he takes that view and finesses in diamonds, he loses the contract.

When a defender can see that a finesse will succeed for

declarer, it will sometimes pay – for deceptive reasons – to contribute the honour. Holding K J x in front of dummy's A Q 10 x, for example, playing the king may deflect declarer from taking a subsequent finesse of the 10.

A very pretty play of this kind was first described by the American writer, Robert Ewen.

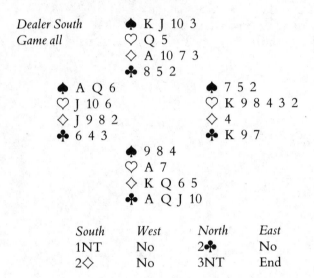

Dealer South　　　　♠ K J 10 3
Game all　　　　　　♡ Q 5
　　　　　　　　　　◇ A 10 7 3
　　　　　　　　　　♣ 8 5 2

♠ A Q 6　　　　　　　　　　　　♠ 7 5 2
♡ J 10 6　　　　　　　　　　　♡ K 9 8 4 3 2
◇ J 9 8 2　　　　　　　　　　◇ 4
♣ 6 4 3　　　　　　　　　　　♣ K 9 7

　　　　　　　　　　♠ 9 8 4
　　　　　　　　　　♡ A 7
　　　　　　　　　　◇ K Q 6 5
　　　　　　　　　　♣ A Q J 10

South	West	North	East
1NT	No	2♣	No
2◇	No	3NT	End

West made the happy lead of the jack of hearts, covered by the queen and king and ducked by South. Back came ♡ 4 to declarer's ace, West unblocking the 10. Clearly South could not afford to lose the lead. He had to take nine tricks in a hurry.

Hoping to make four tricks in each minor, he began with the king and queen of diamonds. As South had denied four cards in either major and had turned up with a doubleton heart (otherwise he would have held off for another round), West could place him with eight cards in the minors, probably 4–4. The finesse against the jack of diamonds would become marked anyhow, so West tried the effect of dropping this card on the second round.

Declarer could now visualize three entries to dummy in the diamond suit, which would let him pick up ♣ K x x x with East. He overtook the queen of diamonds with the ace and could no longer make the contract.

Had West not found this imaginative ploy, declarer would have racked up nine tricks in quick time. Since East had only three clubs to the king, two diamond entries to dummy would suffice.

Yet another technique for the artful defender is 'pretending to be squeezed'. When you have nothing higher than a 7 left in your hand, it can be very off-putting for declarer if you spend thirty seconds deciding which valueless card to throw. Many a contract has been beaten in this way.

No, that's not quite what we had in mind! We were thinking of imaginative efforts like this one, by Lindquist of Sweden in the European Championship at Lausanne.

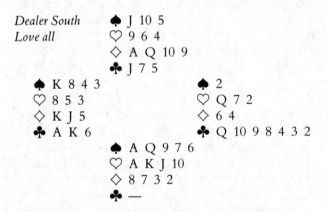

Dealer South
Love all

	♠ J 10 5	
	♡ 9 6 4	
	◇ A Q 10 9	
	♣ J 7 5	
♠ K 8 4 3		♠ 2
♡ 8 5 3		♡ Q 7 2
◇ K J 5		◇ 6 4
♣ A K 6		♣ Q 10 9 8 4 3 2
	♠ A Q 9 7 6	
	♡ A K J 10	
	◇ 8 7 3 2	
	♣ —	

Lindquist led the king of clubs against four spades by South. Declarer ruffed, finessed the diamond queen successfully, and ran the jack of trumps. When Lindquist held off, declarer continued with a low spade to the queen and king. The defence continued clubs and South, to maintain trump control, discarded two diamonds on the ace and queen of clubs. These cards were left:

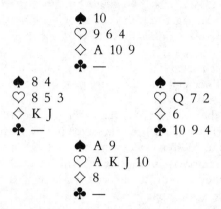

```
                    ♠ 10
                    ♡ 9 6 4
                    ◇ A 10 9
                    ♣ —
    ♠ 8 4                          ♠ —
    ♡ 8 5 3                        ♡ Q 7 2
    ◇ K J                          ◇ 6
    ♣ —                            ♣ 10 9 4
                    ♠ A 9
                    ♡ A K J 10
                    ◇ 8
                    ♣ —
```

Realizing that a ruff-and-discard would not assist the declarer, East played another club. South discarded a heart and took the force in dummy. All that is needed now, as can be seen, is a heart finesse. But . . .

On the fourth round of clubs Lindquist, West, did not discard a heart. He underruffed, playing a low spade in front of dummy's 10. This gave South the impression that West held ♡ Q x x and was retaining a guard in both red suits. Accordingly he came to hand with the heart ace and played off two trumps, thinking that West would be squeezed in the red suits and that after a heart discard the king of hearts would bring down the queen. The queen refused to appear until the last trick and declarer was one down.

It is possible to fault South's reading of the situation because if East had held nothing in hearts he might have exited in diamonds to break up the squeeze. This does not detract from Lindquist's fine effort, of course.

Finally, we turn to a piece of trickery by declarer. The editor of French magazine *Le Bridgeur* described it as machiavellian. It was, too, if declarer foresaw what was going to happen.

Dealer North
Love all

	♠ 7 6 3	
	♡ 9 7 5	
	◇ A 4	
	♣ K 8 7 6 4	

♠ 10 5 4		♠ A K J 8 2
♡ 8 2		♡ A 3
◇ K 10 8 5 2		◇ J 9 6 3
♣ Q 5 2		♣ J 9

	♠ Q 9	
	♡ K Q J 10 6 4	
	◇ Q 7	
	♣ A 10 3	

South	*West*	*North*	*East*
Abécassis	Calix	Perron	Delmouly
—	—	No	1♠
2♡	No	3♡	No
4♡	End		

South's four hearts, as he readily admitted, was a dubious call. The queen of spades was unlikely to pull any weight and North, if strong, would have bid two spades and supported the hearts later.

The defence began with three rounds of spades, South ruffing. As you see, he had only eight tricks on top. If he played on trumps and East returned a diamond, he would finish two down.

Abécassis made a remarkable play. He led a club to the king and played a trump from dummy. It seemed to Delmouly that South must hold ♡ K J 10 x x x, so he went up with the ace of trumps and played a fourth spade, expecting to promote a trick for partner's trump queen.

The expectation was not fulfilled. Declarer discarded a

club, ruffed in dummy, and played off all the trumps, eventually squeezing West in the minor suits.

One could spend a lifetime hoping to achieve such a coup. Worth waiting for, though.

6

Twist in the tail

In boxing it is often necessary to soften your opponent with a few good punches to the body. Only then will his guard drop, allowing a knock-out blow to be delivered.

It is much the same when you are preparing an opponent for a throw-in. Your first move may be to exhaust him of safe exit cards. But when you move in for the kill, beware! The supposedly helpless victim, who you imagined was down to ♠ A ◇ K x, may deliver a lethal counterpunch, emerging with ♠ A x ◇ K instead.

On the following deal, from a Vanderbilt semifinal, West received a nasty shock of a different sort – during the bidding.

```
Dealer East          ♠ Q 6 5 4 3
Game all             ♡ 10
                     ◇ Q J 6 5 2
                     ♣ J 5
♠ 10 2                              ♠ A K J 9 8
♡ Q J 7 4 3 2                       ♡ A 5
◇ A 9 7 4 3                         ◇ 8
♣ —                                ♣ 10 9 8 3 2
                     ♠ 7
                     ♡ K 9 8 6
                     ◇ K 10
                     ♣ A K Q 7 6 4
```

South	West	North	East
Hamilton	Bluhm	Rubin	Sanders
—	—	—	1♠
2♣	Dble	End	

63

West's choice of a negative double on the first round appears somewhat foolish, but perhaps two hearts would not have been forcing in his system. It must have been an unnerving moment when the double was left in by his partner.

East overtook the spade lead and switched to ♣ 10, won in the dummy. When a heart was played, East stepped in with the ace and led ♣ 9. The best line for South now is to continue trumps. When East wins with ♣ 8 he exits with a diamond. South plays the king and West holds off. These cards remain:

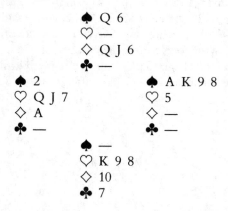

West is put in with the ace of diamonds and, if he has managed to retain a spade, can exit safely in that suit. This only delays the fatal moment. Declarer leads ♡ 9 from hand and West must surrender the last two heart tricks.

Good card-reading was required on that deal, but nothing special by way of preparation. More typical are the hands that involve some degree of elimination. The defender's safe exit cards must be prised from him, one by one. Watch declarer at work on this deal:

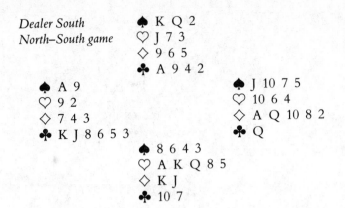

Dealer South
North–South game

North:
♠ K Q 2
♡ J 7 3
◇ 9 6 5
♣ A 9 4 2

West:
♠ A 9
♡ 9 2
◇ 7 4 3
♣ K J 8 6 5 3

East:
♠ J 10 7 5
♡ 10 6 4
◇ A Q 10 8 2
♣ Q

South:
♠ 8 6 4 3
♡ A K Q 8 5
◇ K J
♣ 10 7

South opened one heart and West, in the style that some players think is clever, made a weak jump overcall of three clubs. North might have doubled, but he preferred three hearts and South bid the game.

West made the play a little easier by beginning with ace and another spade. South drew two rounds of trumps, then led a diamond from the table. East went up with the ace and returned his third trump to prevent declarer ruffing the fourth round of spades.

At this point dummy's ◇ 9 is a threat against East, who also controls the fourth round of spades. If declarer could conveniently lose another trick, he would be able to catch East in a criss-cross squeeze. This was hardly a promising line, though. If declarer were to duck a club, either a spade or a diamond return would break up the entries for a squeeze.

South found another resource. Since West had not led a club at trick 1, it seemed a near certainty that East had a singleton honour in the suit. If West's diamonds could be stripped, surely he could be endplayed in the club suit.

Having reached this conclusion, declarer cashed the king of diamonds and crossed to the ace of clubs to ruff dummy's last diamond. West had only clubs remaining in this end position:

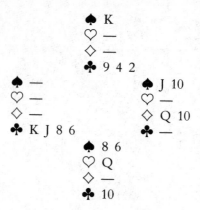

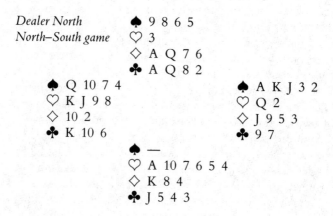

The ♣ 10 to West's jack gave the defenders their third trick, but West had to concede a trick to dummy's ♣ 9. Not a complicated ending, but somehow easy to miss.

We stay with the same theme – removing the defender's exit cards – on the next deal. It was played by the Polish star, Bolek Orlovsky, in a Swiss Teams event in Amsterdam.

Dealer North
North–South game

♠ 9 8 6 5
♡ 3
◇ A Q 7 6
♣ A Q 8 2

♠ Q 10 7 4
♡ K J 9 8
◇ 10 2
♣ K 10 6

♠ A K J 3 2
♡ Q 2
◇ J 9 5 3
♣ 9 7

♠ —
♡ A 10 7 6 5 4
◇ K 8 4
♣ J 5 4 3

South	West	North	East
—	—	1◇	1♠
2♡	2♣	No	No
4♡[1]	Dble	End	

[1] Reckoning that a slam is unlikely after partner's pass, Orlovsky signs off in game(!).

Declarer ruffed the spade lead, led a low heart and ruffed the spade return. He now cashed the ace of hearts, discarding a *club* from dummy. The two remaining spades would be needed later.

Orlovsky finessed the club queen and ruffed a third spade. He then crossed to a diamond and ruffed a fourth spade, removing West's last card in the suit. Had he thrown one of dummy's spades earlier, he would not have been able to extract West's fourth spade.

The king of diamonds was now cashed, leaving these cards still to be played:

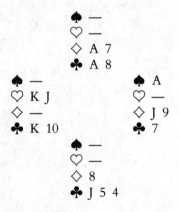

Declarer played another diamond and West could make only his two trump tricks.

Although this was a fine performance by the Pole, it

should be noted that the defenders twice assisted him in his mission to ruff four spades in hand. If West's trumps had been less solid, such as K J 4 2 or A Q 5 3, a forcing defence would have been an attractive proposition. The aim would be to promote his small trumps. When the defender's trump holding is stronger, such as K J 9 8 or A Q 10 6, there is always the risk that a forcing defence will allow declarer to score his small trumps and possibly move towards a coup in the endgame. Had West started with a diamond on his deal, the contract could not have been made.

Loser-on-loser plays are always attractive. You swap one loser for another, hoping that the defender put on lead will advance your cause in one way or another. On the next deal, from a pairs event in Wales, declarer's aim was to establish a safe route back to hand.

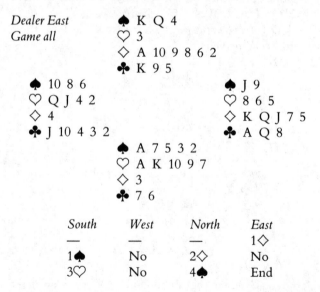

Dealer East
Game all

		♠ K Q 4	
		♡ 3	
		♢ A 10 9 8 6 2	
		♣ K 9 5	
♠ 10 8 6			♠ J 9
♡ Q J 4 2			♡ 8 6 5
♢ 4			♢ K Q J 7 5
♣ J 10 4 3 2			♣ A Q 8
		♠ A 7 5 3 2	
		♡ A K 10 9 7	
		♢ 3	
		♣ 7 6	

South	West	North	East
—	—	—	1♢
1♠	No	2♢	No
3♡	No	4♠	End

West led his singleton diamond, won by dummy's ace. If declarer plays in straightforward fashion – ♡ A, heart ruff, ♠ K Q – he will run into a trump promotion unless he finds West with only two trumps.

A better shot, not easy to see, is to play ◇ 10 from dummy at trick 2, discarding a club from hand. East does best to return a trump, but you win in dummy and play another diamond, discarding your last club. That leaves East on lead in this position:

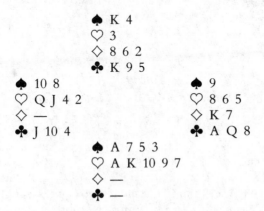

```
              ♠ K 4
              ♡ 3
              ◇ 8 6 2
              ♣ K 9 5
  ♠ 10 8                    ♠ 9
  ♡ Q J 4 2                 ♡ 8 6 5
  ◇ —                       ◇ K 7
  ♣ J 10 4                  ♣ A Q 8
              ♠ A 7 5 3
              ♡ A K 10 9 7
              ◇ —
              ♣ —
```

You can cope with any return from East. If he leads a trump or a heart you will be able to ruff a heart and return to hand with a club ruff to pull the last trump. A long heart will provide your tenth trick. If instead he tries the king of diamonds, you ruff low and make the rest after West has overruffed. If he returns ◇ 7, you discard a heart and subsequently establish dummy's sixth diamond.

When this hand was played, several declarers had the idea of discarding a club on a diamond, but they did it *after* they had taken a heart ruff. Too late! Since one entry to dummy (the heart ruff) had been used prematurely, the long diamonds no longer posed a threat.

The next deal is similar at first glance. You can ruff one of your losers quite easily, but there is no quick route back to hand.

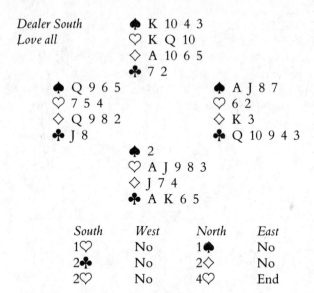

Dealer South ♠ K 10 4 3
Love all   ♡ K Q 10
      ♢ A 10 6 5
      ♣ 7 2

♠ Q 9 6 5   ♠ A J 8 7
♡ 7 5 4   ♡ 6 2
♢ Q 9 8 2   ♢ K 3
♣ J 8   ♣ Q 10 9 4 3

      ♠ 2
      ♡ A J 9 8 3
      ♢ J 7 4
      ♣ A K 6 5

South	West	North	East
1♡	No	1♠	No
2♣	No	2♢	No
2♡	No	4♡	End

West was short in declarer's side suit and therefore decided to lead a trump. (Many players, quite wrongly, are more inclined to lead a trump when they are *long* in declarer's side suit. In that case there is always the chance that if declarer plays for ruffs your partner will be able to overruff the dummy.)

In four hearts South won the trump lead, cashed two rounds of clubs and took a club ruff. Thanks to the accurate opening lead, prospects of a second club ruff were bleak. Declarer turned his mind to a possible throw-in, with East the victim. He drew three more rounds of trumps to arrive at this end position:

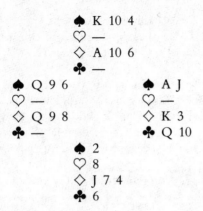

```
              ♠ K 10 4
              ♡ —
              ♢ A 10 6
              ♣ —
♠ Q 9 6                    ♠ A J
♡ —                        ♡ —
♢ Q 9 8                    ♢ K 3
♣ —                        ♣ Q 10
              ♠ 2
              ♡ 8
              ♢ J 7 4
              ♣ 6
```

Declarer now led ♣ 6, discarding a spade from dummy. When East returned another club, a spade was thrown from the South hand and a diamond from North. East had no good exit. If he led the jack of spades, declarer would simply discard a diamond, not caring which defender held the spade ace.

Nothing the defenders could do on that last hand, but there are many throw-in plays which can be prevented. Or declarer can be put to a guess at any rate. Imagine that you are East in this end position:

```
              ♠ K 6
              ♡ A Q
              ♢ —
              ♣ 6 4
                           ♠ A 10 7
                           ♡ K J 2
immaterial                 ♢ —
                           ♣ —
              ♠ 4
              ♡ 9 8
              ♢ —
              ♣ Q J 10
```

Declarer, who can place you with the high cards because of an earlier bid, cashes three rounds of clubs, throwing a spade from dummy. What is your best sequence of discards?

In normal circumstances you will do best to throw ♡ 2, ♡ J, then ♠ 10. Mind you, if South is an expert and has a high regard for your own play, he may *expect* you to bare the heart king. In that case a double-bluff would be in order. You might try the effect of ♡ J, followed by ♠ 7 and ♠ 10.

West bared a king to good effect on this deal from rubber bridge:

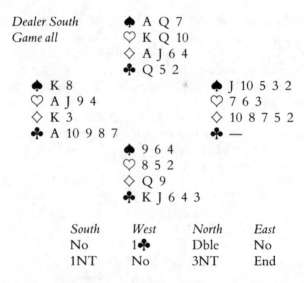

Dealer South   ♠ A Q 7
Game all   ♡ K Q 10
               ◇ A J 6 4
               ♣ Q 5 2

♠ K 8   ♠ J 10 5 3 2
♡ A J 9 4   ♡ 7 6 3
◇ K 3   ◇ 10 8 7 5 2
♣ A 10 9 8 7   ♣ —

               ♠ 9 6 4
               ♡ 8 5 2
               ◇ Q 9
               ♣ K J 6 4 3

South	West	North	East
No	1♣	Dble	No
1NT	No	3NT	End

West led ♣ 10 to South's jack, and a heart to the king was followed by a diamond to the 9 and king. West exited safely in diamonds and declarer played a second round of hearts towards dummy. West rose with the ace and exited with a mildly deceptive jack of hearts.

When dummy's ◇ A J were cashed, West threw ♠ 8

72

and a club. The lead was in dummy with these cards remaining:

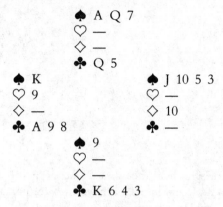

♠ A Q 7
♡ —
♢ —
♣ Q 5

♠ K   ♠ J 10 5 3
♡ 9   ♡ —
♢ —   ♢ 10
♣ A 9 8   ♣ —

♠ 9
♡ —
♢ —
♣ K 6 4 3

The queen of clubs was led, West holding off. Declarer, who at this stage placed West with ♠ K x ♣ A 9, played another club, expecting to win the last two tricks in spades. West cashed two clubs, then surprised declarer by producing ♡ 9. The game was one down.

West defended cleverly, but declarer should have made the contract all the same. When the queen of clubs is allowed to win, he should cash the ace of spades. If West is indeed down to ♠ K x ♣ A 9, he can be thrown in with a spade to give declarer a third club trick.

Another defensive weapon against the throw-in is the unblock. By releasing high cards early in the play, you avoid being thrown in with them later when the pressure is on. Here is Garozzo at work in the American Blue Ribbon Pairs:

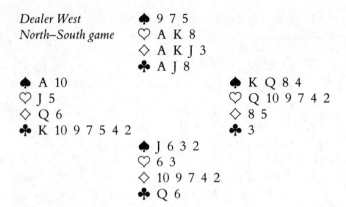

Dealer West
North–South game

North:
♠ 9 7 5
♡ A K 8
♢ A K J 3
♣ A J 8

West:
♠ A 10
♡ J 5
♢ Q 6
♣ K 10 9 7 5 4 2

East:
♠ K Q 8 4
♡ Q 10 9 7 4 2
♢ 8 5
♣ 3

South:
♠ J 6 3 2
♡ 6 3
♢ 10 9 7 4 2
♣ Q 6

Garozzo, who held the West cards, opened 3 NT, presumably a pre-empt in one of the minors (or perhaps in *any* suit). The bidding continued:

South	West	North	East
—	3NT	Dble	4♣[1]
No	No	Dble	No
4♢	No	5♢	End

[1] To pass would imply that East could stand 3 NT. He rescues into the low suit, expecting West to remove to diamonds if that is his suit.

West led a heart against five diamonds. South drew trumps, eliminated the hearts and led the club queen, covered by the king and ace. After jack of clubs and a club ruff, the position was:

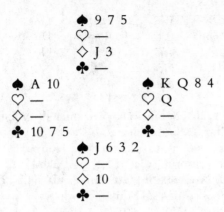

♠ 9 7 5
♡ —
♢ J 3
♣ —

♠ A 10 ♠ K Q 8 4
♡ — ♡ Q
♢ — ♢ —
♣ 10 7 5 ♣ —

♠ J 6 3 2
♡ —
♢ 10
♣ —

South, one of America's top players, led a low spade with a nonchalant air, but of course Garozzo went up with the ace and led another spade. At fifty tables no one else made a plus score on the East–West cards.

The defender in the West seat faced a similar problem on the next hand, from an England–France clash in a Common Market championship.

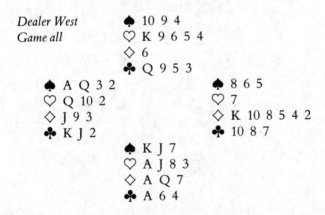

Dealer West
Game all

♠ 10 9 4
♡ K 9 6 5 4
♢ 6
♣ Q 9 5 3

♠ A Q 3 2 ♠ 8 6 5
♡ Q 10 2 ♡ 7
♢ J 9 3 ♢ K 10 8 5 4 2
♣ K J 2 ♣ 10 8 7

♠ K J 7
♡ A J 8 3
♢ A Q 7
♣ A 6 4

South	West	North	East
Chemla	Price	Reiplinger	Duckworth
—	1♣	No	No
2NT	No	3♣[1]	No
3♡	No	4♡	End

[1] Stayman. Had South responded three diamonds, North would have bid three hearts to show a five-card suit. A better scheme is to play transfers opposite notrump overcalls, ensuring that the strong hand will play the contract. Note that if four hearts is played by North on this deal, a spade lead beats the contract.

As it was, South became declarer and West led a diamond to the king and ace. Chemla discarded a spade on the diamond queen and ruffed a diamond. He then played three rounds of trumps, putting West on lead. West had to choose his exit card with care in this end position:

```
              ♠ 10 9
              ♡ 9
              ◇ —
              ♣ Q 9 5 3
♠ A Q 3 2                    ♠ 8 6 5
♡ —                         ♡ —
◇ —                         ◇ 10
♣ K J 2                     ♣ 10 8 7
              ♠ K J 7
              ♡ 8
              ◇ —
              ♣ A 6 4
```

West played the jack of clubs, won by dummy's queen. On the next club West dropped the king under declarer's ace. Now his partner was able to win the third round of clubs and play a spade through declarer's spade tenace. The contract went one down.

Some commentators declared that the jack of clubs was the only exit card to defeat the contract. In fact the king of clubs is just as good – so long as West rises with the jack when a second round of clubs is led towards the dummy.

The club holding looks ordinary, but it gives rise to some interesting problems. Suppose the ace of clubs is led by declarer at trick 2. West must unblock the king, because otherwise South may (in theory) develop the clubs early on and endplay West on the third round of trumps.

More interesting, suppose declarer leads a *low* club at trick 2, West must play the *jack* on this lead and later throw the king under the ace; otherwise, he will be on play after the third round of clubs.

A rather pretty echo of this deal occurred in a rubber game at the St John's Wood Club. The spotlight again fell on the West player.

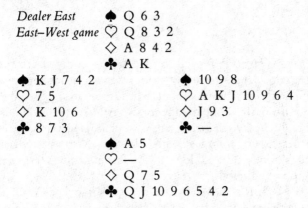

Dealer East — East–West game

	♠ Q 6 3	
	♡ Q 8 3 2	
	◇ A 8 4 2	
	♣ A K	
♠ K J 7 4 2		♠ 10 9 8
♡ 7 5		♡ A K J 10 9 6 4
◇ K 10 6		◇ J 9 3
♣ 8 7 3		♣ —
	♠ A 5	
	♡ —	
	◇ Q 7 5	
	♣ Q J 10 9 6 5 4 2	

East opened three hearts and South overcalled four clubs. West passed and North could think of nothing better than a raise to six clubs, which was passed all round. West led a heart to the jack and South ruffed.

Declarer could count ten top tricks, with an eleventh surely available from dummy's queen of spades. As for a twelfth trick, it seemed as if West might have some difficulty in avoiding an endplay. Declarer's first step was to extract West's hearts. He crossed to the king of clubs, ruffed a heart high, returned to the ace of clubs and ruffed another heart high. He then ran the trump suit, leading to this end position:

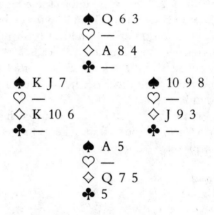

On the last club West discarded ♠ 7, dummy and East a diamond. When the ace of spades was led, it looked for a moment as if West was about to be thrown in and forced to lead from the king of diamonds. After a few seconds' thought he avoided this fate by unblocking the king of spades. South followed with a low spade to West's jack and skilfully played low from dummy. So West was endplayed after all.

West stirred his grey matter a trick too late. Had he made the unusual play of discarding the jack of spades on declarer's last trump, he could have followed by dropping the king under declarer's ace. His partner's spades would then be promoted to the front line, killing all chance of an endplay.

West had a chance to impress on the next hand, too. See if you can spot the opportunity he missed.

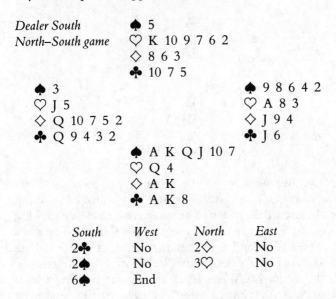

		Dealer South		
		♠ 5		
		♡ K 10 9 7 6 2		
North–South game		♢ 8 6 3		
		♣ 10 7 5		

♠ 3		♠ 9 8 6 4 2
♡ J 5		♡ A 8 3
♢ Q 10 7 5 2		♢ J 9 4
♣ Q 9 4 3 2		♣ J 6

♠ A K Q J 10 7
♡ Q 4
♢ A K
♣ A K 8

South	West	North	East
2♣	No	2♢	No
2♠	No	3♡	No
6♠	End		

The leap to six spades was certainly tempting, although one knows from experience that while partners sometimes have what they promise, they seldom have what one hopes.

A diamond was led, won in the South hand. Dummy must have been quite a disappointment, but declarer kept his wits about him. He drew trumps in five rounds, throwing three hearts and a club from dummy (he had plans for dummy's third diamond). Next he cashed his other diamond winner and led ♡ 4, finessing dummy's 10.

Since West would obviously have split his honours if he held ♡ Q J x, East could place declarer with another heart. He therefore had to hold off the heart ace. Dummy's ♡ 10 won the trick and these cards remained:

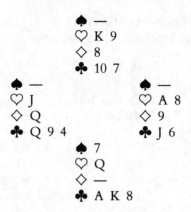

```
              ♠ —
              ♡ K 9
              ◇ 8
              ♣ 10 7
  ♠ —                      ♠ —
  ♡ J                      ♡ A 8
  ◇ Q                      ◇ 9
  ♣ Q 9 4                  ♣ J 6
              ♠ 7
              ♡ Q
              ◇ —
              ♣ A K 8
```

Declarer now ruffed the carefully preserved ◇ 8, removing East's last card in the suit. He cashed the two top clubs and led the queen of hearts, covered by the jack, king and ace. East stared at his last card (♡ 8) and at dummy's last card (♡ 9) and gave a resigned shrug of the shoulders.

Declarer was lucky to find West with J x in hearts, and lucky again that West played low on the first heart lead. Had West thought to insert the jack, forcing dummy's king, East could have blocked the suit by winning with the ace. Declarer would then have had no parking place for his club loser.

We end the chapter with a spectacular hand from a pairs tournament in Vienna:

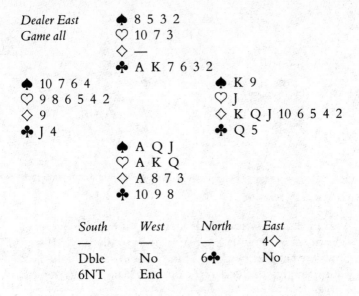

Dealer East
Game all

♠ 8 5 3 2
♡ 10 7 3
♢ —
♣ A K 7 6 3 2

♠ 10 7 6 4
♡ 9 8 6 5 4 2
♢ 9
♣ J 4

♠ K 9
♡ J
♢ K Q J 10 6 5 4 2
♣ Q 5

♠ A Q J
♡ A K Q
♢ A 8 7 3
♣ 10 9 8

South	West	North	East
—	—	—	4♢
Dble	No	6♣	No
6NT	End		

Six clubs, made with an overtrick, would have been quite a good score for North–South, but the Austrian declarer could not resist 6 NT.

A diamond was led, won by South, and the obvious problem was the blockage in clubs. If clubs were 2–2 and West held a singleton diamond and ♠ K x x, it might be possible to give up a spade and later discard the blocking club on dummy's thirteenth spade. That line did not appeal to the declarer, who was somewhat of an eccentric by nature. He won the diamond lead, throwing a *club* from dummy, then crossed to the ace of clubs and took a successful spade finesse. The ace and jack of spades were followed by the top two hearts, bringing down the jack. After a club to the king the position was:

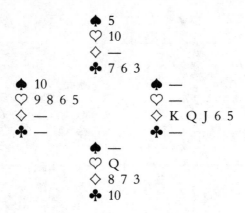

```
                    ♠ 5
                    ♡ 10
                    ◇ —
                    ♣ 7 6 3
♠ 10                                    ♠ —
♡ 9 8 6 5                               ♡ —
◇ —                                     ◇ K Q J 6 5
♣ —                                     ♣ —
                    ♠ —
                    ♡ Q
                    ◇ 8 7 3
                    ♣ 10
```

On dummy's last spade declarer threw the queen of hearts. West now had to play a heart to dummy's 10 and away went the blocking club. Dummy was high. Not surprisingly, the declarer won a brilliancy prize for his play.

Well, did you believe all that? Some people will believe anything they read in a book. A real-life declarer would play the hand quite differently. Provided West has a single-ton diamond and East has the spade king, you can make the contract much more simply (and with a far greater likelihood of success) by ducking a club to West. This will be possible whenever West holds ♣ Q singleton, ♣ Q x, or any three clubs.

So, the best line is to discard a heart from dummy at trick 1, cross to the ace of clubs and finesse the spade. Then you play a second round of clubs, ducking when West's jack appears. You go seven down vulnerable as the cards lie, of course. But at least you will have played the hand correctly – that's the main thing.

7

Avoiding the blind spot

It is very rare for top-class players to make an absurd blunder, and when they do you can be sure that the event will be well publicized. It is the nature of the beast that snippets such as *'the Italian defender unaccountably failed to cash the ace of clubs before . . . '* make very palatable reading.

In this chapter you can try your luck on several deals where players of the top rank had a blind spot. Here's the first one. If it's not too early in the day, cover the East–West cards and have a go at 6 NT. West leads ♡ 9.

Dealer South
Love all

	♠ A J 4	
	♡ A K J 2	
	◇ J 7 6 2	
	♣ K 9	

♠ K 7 3		♠ Q 9 8 5
♡ 9 8 6		♡ 10 7 5 3
◇ K 10 8 4		◇ 5
♣ 10 7 3		♣ 8 6 5 2

	♠ 10 6 2	
	♡ Q 4	
	◇ A Q 9 3	
	♣ A Q J 4	

South	West	North	East
1NT[1]	No	2♣	No
2◇	No	6NT[2]	End

[1] 15–17.

[2] A natural 4 NT would be more accurate, but it was a pairs and North thought his side needed a top.

West led ♡ 9, won in the South hand. Having escaped a spade lead, declarer was delighted with his contract. Three diamond tricks would bring the total to twelve and since the combined point-count was a slender 32 an excellent board was in prospect. Celebrating prematurely, declarer crossed to the king of clubs and finessed the queen of diamonds. The slam could no longer be made.

Correct play is to cash the ace of diamonds at trick 2 and lead a low diamond towards the jack. If East has ♢ K 10 x x you will still score three tricks in the suit. When West has the long diamonds, as in the actual layout, he cannot afford to go in with the king. Dummy's jack wins and East shows out.

Declarer now has eleven tricks and must aim for a spade-diamond squeeze on West. An early finesse of ♠ J will not work well because East can return a spade to break the squeeze. Instead declarer should cash four rounds of hearts, discarding two diamonds from hand, then embark on the club suit. This will be the end position:

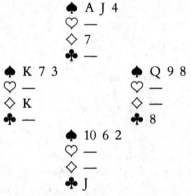

```
              ♠ A J 4
              ♡ —
              ♢ 7
              ♣ —
  ♠ K 7 3              ♠ Q 9 8
  ♡ —                  ♡ —
  ♢ K                  ♢ —
  ♣ —                  ♣ 8
              ♠ 10 6 2
              ♡ —
              ♢ —
              ♣ J
```

The jack of clubs is played and West must discard a spade. Dummy throws ♢ 7 and now a spade to the jack brings declarer two spade tricks.

Players who tend to take optimistic views in the bidding

may need to take good views in the play. South failed to justify his forward bidding on the next deal. See if you would have done any better; the contract is six spades on a heart lead.

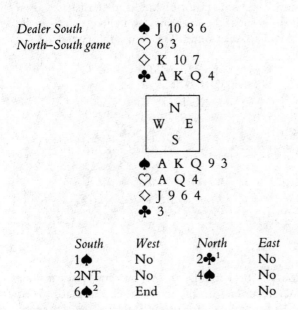

Dealer South
North–South game

♠ J 10 8 6
♡ 6 3
♢ K 10 7
♣ A K Q 4

♠ A K Q 9 3
♡ A Q 4
♢ J 9 6 4
♣ 3

South	West	North	East
1♠	No	2♣[1]	No
2NT	No	4♠	No
6♠[2]	End		No

[1] Under strength for a force, North plans a delayed game raise.
[2] Many players would laboriously show the heart control, simply averting what might be a favourable lead.

A heart is led to the king and ace. You draw trumps in two rounds, cash the queen of hearts and ruff a heart. On this trick East discards a diamond. You now cash the three top clubs, discarding two diamonds from hand. When you play a fourth round of clubs, East discards another diamond. You ruff in hand, leaving yourself with ♠ Q 9 ♢ J 9 opposite dummy's ♠ J ♢ K 10 7. Obviously the contract will depend on your taking a correct view of the diamond suit.

When you have eventually made up your mind you lead the nine of diamonds and . . . horror of horrors . . . West shows out! That's the point of the hand. East has shown precisely two spades, two hearts and three clubs, so he must hold all six diamonds. This is the full layout:

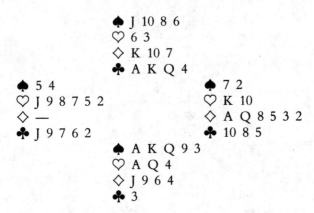

Do you see the winning play? You must discard your penultimate diamond on the fourth round of clubs. West will then have to give you a ruff-and-discard. Easy to miss, because you have to switch direction suddenly, when in midstream.

There was nothing very difficult about the key play on the next deal and the player who missed it was so upset at the time that he declared he would never again enter an international trial. Funny, his name was in the line-up only a couple of weeks later.

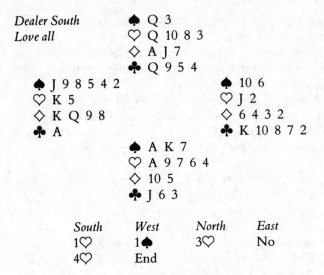

Dealer South	♠ Q 3		
Love all	♡ Q 10 8 3		
	◇ A J 7		
	♣ Q 9 5 4		

♠ J 9 8 5 4 2   ♠ 10 6
♡ K 5   ♡ J 2
◇ K Q 9 8   ◇ 6 4 3 2
♣ A   ♣ K 10 8 7 2

♠ A K 7
♡ A 9 7 6 4
◇ 10 5
♣ J 6 3

South	West	North	East
1♡	1♠	3♡	No
4♡	End		

South had little justification for advancing over his partner's limit bid and the resultant contract was a poor one. Hands with a 5–3–3–2 distribution, cousin to 4–3–3–3, are generally unproductive. As it happens, 3 NT is a reasonable game, but this is hard to reach.

West led the king of diamonds against four hearts. Declarer won with the ace and returned a diamond to the 10 and queen. When West cashed the ace of clubs and exited with a diamond, it was evident that the ace of clubs was a singleton. Declarer saw that if he could eliminate the spades he might be able to endplay West with ace and another trump. He cashed the ace of trumps and followed with the three top spades, but on the third round his plan went sadly astray. East ruffed and cashed the king of clubs, putting the contract two down.

'Sorry, partner,' said South. 'I should have passed three hearts. I had a pretty awful 12-count.'

'You could have made it, couldn't you?' replied North.

'Just ruff the third round of spades with the queen before exiting with a trump.'

South might well have found this play. West had over-called in a suit that was at best jack high, so it was quite likely that he had six of them.

Would you think it possible that six international players – not to mention the *Bulletin* editor – could all have the same blind spot? Apparently they can, if you look at this deal from the round robin of a world championship.

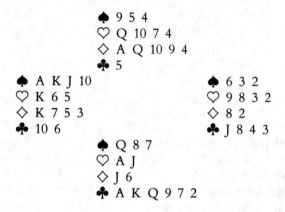

The contract at all six tables – there were three matches in play – was 3 NT by South. In every case West opened a high spade and switched to a diamond.

The first decision the various declarers faced was whether to finesse in diamonds. If the finesse lost, the defenders would surely cash enough spade tricks to beat the contract. Still, rising with the ace was likely to be a good idea only if the clubs were coming in *and* the heart finesse was right.

Two declarers did decide to go up with the diamond ace and then take the heart finesse. Borin, sitting West for Australia, found the good defence of cashing the king of diamonds and exiting with a heart. Now South had no entry to dummy. The other declarer who followed this line succeeded because of a defensive error.

Belladonna tried a different line. At trick 2 he let the diamond run to his jack, then he cashed the top clubs. When they failed to break, he finessed ◇ 9, cashed the ace, and exited with a diamond. West cleared the spades and declarer was a trick short. Two other declarers took this line, one succeeding when the defence was mistimed.

Cummings, for Australia, won the second trick with ◇ 9 and followed with the ace and jack of hearts. When West ducked, he cashed the top clubs, took two diamonds and exited with a heart, forcing West to give him his ninth trick with the queen of spades. This was a reasonable line of play after West had doubled the opening bid.

Well, what was the line they all missed? Once declarer had put in ◇ 9 at trick 2, which is certainly better than letting it run to the jack, all he need do is make an elementary avoidance play in clubs. He plays a low club to the 9, and unless the clubs are 5–1 (or East inserts an honour from ♣ J 10 x x), he is assured of five clubs, three diamonds and a heart. If the clubs prove disappointing, the other chances remain.

When a contract appears almost impossible most players are willing to apply themselves to the search for some line that may succeed. It requires more discipline to make just the same effort when a contract will be easy on normal breaks. One of Australia's top stars took a substandard line on this deal from a Bermuda Bowl match. The cards did not forgive him. The misplay cost 29 IMPs!

Dealer West　　　　　♠ A K J 7
Game all　　　　　　♡ K 10 4 3
　　　　　　　　　　♢ 9 5
　　　　　　　　　　♣ A Q 8

♠ 8 5 3　　　　　　　　　　　　♠ 10 2
♡ Q 9 8 5 2　　　　　　　　　　♡ J 7 6
♢ Q 10 8 6　　　　　　　　　　♢ K J 4 2
♣ 5　　　　　　　　　　　　　　♣ J 10 4 2

　　　　　　　　　　♠ Q 9 6 4
　　　　　　　　　　♡ A
　　　　　　　　　　♢ A 7 3
　　　　　　　　　　♣ K 9 7 6 3

South	West	North	East
—	No	1NT	No
2NT[1]	No	3♣	No
3♠[2]	No	4NT[3]	No
5♡	No	7♠	End

[1] A transfer, showing a club suit.

[2] Indicating a good hand, with spades as well as clubs.

[3] Well judged, though it is unusual for a player who has opened with a limit bid to take control of the auction.

West led a heart against seven spades. Declarer won with the ace, crossed to a trump and ruffed a heart. He then drew trumps and played on clubs. They failed to break 3–2 and the slam went one down.

When declarer returned to dummy after the first ruff, he could see that the trumps were breaking 3–2. It was therefore safe to take a second heart ruff, with the queen, before drawing the last trump. He could then have ruffed the clubs good, cashed the king of hearts and returned to the diamond ace to enjoy the last club.

At the other table North–South stopped in game, bidding 1NT – 2♣; 2♠ – 4♠. Most players appreciate that grand-slam bids in matchplay are a very doubtful proposition if there is any possibility that the opponents may not proceed beyond game. The odds, when vulnerable, may surprise you, nevertheless. By bidding seven instead of six you stand to lose 26 IMPs, to gain just 4.

8

Offbeat squeezes

Bridge writers tend to collect exotic squeezes with the fanaticism of an entomologist in a tropical jungle. Such hands can make interesting reading, but if they turn up only once a century they have little instructive value. The squeezes in this chapter are all slightly unusual in one way or another, but they are real life specimens that were dealt at the table. You will meet their like time and again . . . if you keep your eyes open!

In the first example declarer discards a loser on a loser to make the timing right for a squeeze – one of the most attractive moves in the game. See if you can pick out the critical play.

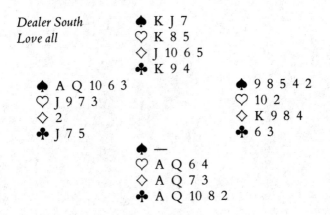

Dealer South
Love all

```
                    ♠ K J 7
                    ♡ K 8 5
                    ♢ J 10 6 5
                    ♣ K 9 4
♠ A Q 10 6 3                        ♠ 9 8 5 4 2
♡ J 9 7 3                           ♡ 10 2
♢ 2                                 ♢ K 9 8 4
♣ J 7 5                             ♣ 6 3
                    ♠ —
                    ♡ A Q 6 4
                    ♢ A Q 7 3
                    ♣ A Q 10 8 2
```

The bidding was not very scientific:

South	West	North	East
1♣	1♠	2NT	No
6♣(!)	End		

South's alternative, over 2 NT, was three diamonds; or perhaps three spades, hoping that his partner could name a suit at the four level. As it happens, six diamonds, played by North, doesn't go well.

Suspecting, perhaps, that declarer might be void in spades, West began with his singleton diamond against six clubs. Dummy's 10 was covered by the king and ace. South drew trumps in three rounds and led a low diamond to the jack, on which West showed out. These cards remained:

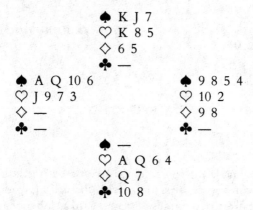

At this point the declarer made the pretty play of leading the jack of spades from dummy, discarding a diamond from hand. By surrendering a trick he improved the timing of the hand. Seven tricks remained and declarer had six winners – an ideal setting for a squeeze.

West won the spade and exited with a heart to the 10 and

queen. Declarer then cashed the queen of diamonds and the last two trumps, squeezing West in the major suits. If East had held four hearts (unlikely), then he would have been squeezed in the red suits.

This hand was a typical example of the simple squeeze. West was unable to guard against a one-card menace (♠ K) and a menace accompanied by a winner (♡ A x x opposite ♡ K x).

It is generally believed that a one-card menace controlled by *both* opponents is valueless except in a guard squeeze (the type where a defender may expose his partner to a finesse). This deal from a Spingold semifinal shows that there are exceptions:

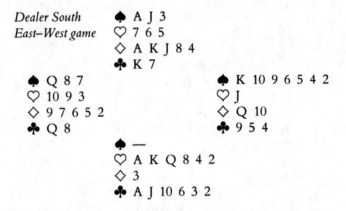

Dealer South
East–West game

	♠ A J 3	
	♡ 7 6 5	
	♢ A K J 8 4	
	♣ K 7	
♠ Q 8 7		♠ K 10 9 6 5 4 2
♡ 10 9 3		♡ J
♢ 9 7 6 5 2		♢ Q 10
♣ Q 8		♣ 9 5 4
	♠ —	
	♡ A K Q 8 4 2	
	♢ 3	
	♣ A J 10 6 3 2	

At one table the contract was a conservative six hearts. After winning the first trick with the ace of spades the declarer drew two rounds of trumps, led a club to the king, and made the safety play of finessing on the way back. Twelve tricks were made.

At the other table North–South reached a red-blooded seven hearts and West led a trump. The declarer drew trumps, played a diamond to dummy, and was able to take three discards (on ♢ K J and ♠ A) when the queen of diamonds fell on the second round. Then he ruffed a spade and drew one more trump, arriving at this end position:

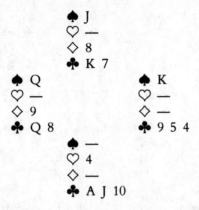

```
              ♠ J
              ♡ —
              ◇ 8
              ♣ K 7
    ♠ Q              ♠ K
    ♡ —              ♡ —
    ◇ 9              ◇ —
    ♣ Q 8            ♣ 9 5 4
              ♠ —
              ♡ 4
              ◇ —
              ♣ A J 10
```

On the last trump West had to discard his queen of spades. A diamond was thrown from dummy, having done good work, and East had to discard a club. South played a club to the king and another club, on which East played the 9. Declarer reasoned that East's thirteenth card must be the king of spades (West would doubtless have led a spade from K Q). He therefore played for the drop in clubs, landing his slam. The jack of spades, you see, played a critical part.

Menace cards are usually more powerful when they lie *over* the defender who has to guard them. The reason for this is clear. The defender will then have to discard before the hand that lies over him. The next hand was unusual in that a squeeze succeeded despite both the one-card menaces lying in front of the defender who guarded them.

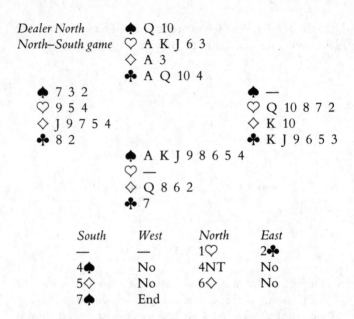

Dealer North
North–South game

North:
♠ Q 10
♡ A K J 6 3
♢ A 3
♣ A Q 10 4

West:
♠ 7 3 2
♡ 9 5 4
♢ J 9 7 5 4
♣ 8 2

East:
♠ —
♡ Q 10 8 7 2
♢ K 10
♣ K J 9 6 5 3

South:
♠ A K J 9 8 6 5 4
♡ —
♢ Q 8 6 2
♣ 7

South	West	North	East
—	—	1♡	2♣
4♠	No	4NT	No
5♢	No	6♢	No
7♠	End		

North's 4 NT was the 'old Black' and six diamonds was a grand slam try. Since his trumps were very long and strong, South advanced to seven.

When West led a club, won by dummy's ace, East was fairly hopeful. He saw that declarer would be unable to establish a long heart; his own defence in diamonds and clubs looked good because he would be discarding after the dummy.

South had twelve tricks on top and it was natural to test the hearts for his thirteenth. He cashed one spade, played ace, king and another heart, then returned to dummy for one more lead of hearts. The news at this point was not good. West showed out and it was evident that no extra trick could be established in the heart suit.

East had been enjoying the hand so far, but after two more rounds of trumps the position was:

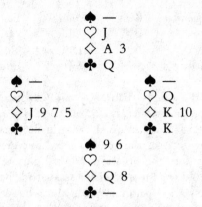

```
              ♠ —
              ♡ J
              ◇ A 3
              ♣ Q
♠ —                      ♠ —
♡ —                      ♡ Q
◇ J 9 7 5                ◇ K 10
♣ —                      ♣ K
              ♠ 9 6
              ♡ —
              ◇ Q 8
              ♣ —
```

South led ♣ 9 and discarded a diamond from the table. Now East found himself squeezed in three suits. As a heart or a club would obviously be fatal, he let go a diamond. South crossed to the ace of diamonds and returned to hand to make the thirteenth trick with the queen of diamonds. It was an unusual type of trump squeeze, made possible by the fact that all the defensive controls were in one hand.

Have you ever picked up a 2-count, heard the bidding opened on your left – and finished as declarer in a slam contract? It happened on this deal between Brazil and Poland during an Olympiad.

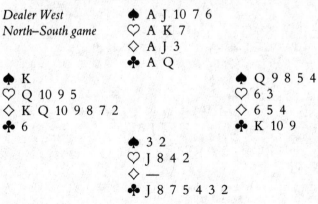

```
Dealer West              ♠ A J 10 7 6
North–South game         ♡ A K 7
                         ◇ A J 3
                         ♣ A Q
♠ K                                    ♠ Q 9 8 5 4
♡ Q 10 9 5                             ♡ 6 3
◇ K Q 10 9 8 7 2                       ◇ 6 5 4
♣ 6                                    ♣ K 10 9
                         ♠ 3 2
                         ♡ J 8 4 2
                         ◇ —
                         ♣ J 8 7 5 4 3 2
```

South	West	North	East
—	1◇	Dble	1♠
No	2◇	Dble	No
4♣	No	6♣	End

West led the king of diamonds and Przybora, the Polish declarer (you guessed it), ruffed the trick. The club finesse lost and a heart was returned, won in dummy. It seems normal now to cash the ace of clubs, but Przybora saw more deeply into the situation. He had only ten tricks on top and would need to establish a spade trick before a red-suit squeeze could operate. What's more, he would need a convenient entry to dummy to cash the spade trick before returning to hand to run the trump suit.

Przybora therefore left the ace of clubs on the table and discarded a spade on the ace of diamonds. He then cashed the ace of spades, dropping West's king, and led the jack. East covered with the queen and declarer ruffed. He now crossed to the carefully preserved ace of clubs to cash ♠ 10. Returning to hand with a spade ruff, he ran the trumps to reach this ending:

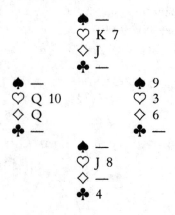

Now West was extinguished by the last trump – a scintillating effort by the Polish star.

Declarer was relying on West holding the queen of hearts on that hand, otherwise there would be no squeeze. It's the same with all squeeze hands. You must assume that the side suits lie in such a way that one (or both) defenders may be brought under pressure.

Making this assumption may lead you to play the trumps in a particular fashion. That's what might have happened on this deal:

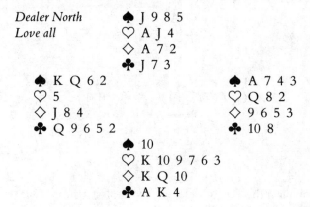

Dealer North ♠ J 9 8 5
Love all ♡ A J 4
  ◇ A 7 2
  ♣ J 7 3

♠ K Q 6 2   ♠ A 7 4 3
♡ 5   ♡ Q 8 2
◇ J 8 4   ◇ 9 6 5 3
♣ Q 9 6 5 2   ♣ 10 8

  ♠ 10
  ♡ K 10 9 7 6 3
  ◇ K Q 10
  ♣ A K 4

Reckoning that his side needed one more big swing to win a short match in the Spring Foursomes, North opened a sub-minimum 1 NT. South soon carried the side to six hearts. When West led the king of spades and continued with a low spade to the ace, South ruffed and played off the ace and king of trumps. No luck there, and a club had to be lost as well.

It transpired that making this slam would have been enough for a dramatic last board win. If declarer takes a certain view of the hand, he does have a chance to make twelve tricks. The odds are heavily against the queen of clubs dropping in two rounds, and it is perhaps better to assume a 5–2 break with the queen in the long hand. If West has the five clubs, in addition to the queen of spades, he can be squeezed.

As for the trump suit, if you are going to play West for four spades and five clubs, it is logical to play him for shortage in hearts. So you begin with ace and jack of hearts. When the jack holds you ruff a spade and play trumps, reaching this position eventually:

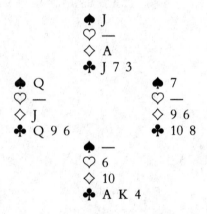

You play the ace of clubs and your last trump. West discards a diamond and dummy a club. Now a diamond to the ace finishes West, who must concede a trick in one or other black suit.

Do you think there could ever be a squeeze in a single suit, without any menace cards? It seems unlikely, but certainly there was an element of pressure in the play of the following hand:

Dealer South ♠ Q 7 6 4 2
East–West game ♡ 8 5
    ◇ 7 4 3
    ♣ A J 10

♠ K   ♠ 10 9 8 3
♡ A K J 7 3   ♡ 10 9 6 4 2
◇ 9 5   ◇ 10 2
♣ 9 7 6 3 2   ♣ 8 5

    ♠ A J 5
    ♡ Q
    ◇ A K Q J 8 6
    ♣ K Q 4

South	West	North	East
2◇¹	No	2♠²	No
4NT	No	5◇	No
6◇	End		

¹ Acol, forcing for one round.
² A dubious effort. Positive responses in a suit that lacks
the ace or king are best avoided.

West led the ace of hearts and followed with the king,
South ruffing. Declarer's only hope, apparently, was to
find East with K x of spades or a singleton king. As there
were no menace cards in the other suits, declarer saw no
point in playing off all the diamonds and clubs, with the
danger of going two down. He put the spade suit to the
test early on and lost to the singleton king.

But see what happens if declarer plays for what might be
called a 'showdown squeeze', since it is similar to a 'show-
up squeeze'. He plays off all the trumps, then three rounds
of clubs. This is the position when the third club is led:

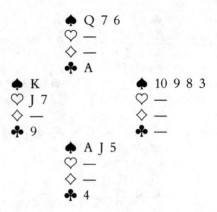

When East discards a spade on this trick, what inference should South draw? Obviously East, with no need to keep any card in hearts, would not have discarded from ♠ K x x. Declarer's *only* chance is to go up with the ace of spades.

If it is ever your fortune to attend a European Championship, we can give you one piece of 'kibitzing' advice: don't watch the Open teams all the time, watch some of the women's matches. The play in the Open tends to be slow and the bidding incomprehensible. In the women's matches, particularly those where the Latin countries are engaged, there is always something of technical and temperamental interest. This hand was played some years ago between Italy and Spain:

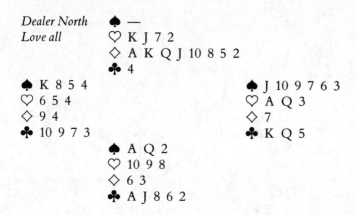

Dealer North
Love all

♠	—
♡	K J 7 2
◇	A K Q J 10 8 5 2
♣	4

♠ K 8 5 4	♠ J 10 9 7 6 3
♡ 6 5 4	♡ A Q 3
◇ 9 4	◇ 7
♣ 10 9 7 3	♣ K Q 5

♠	A Q 2
♡	10 9 8
◇	6 3
♣	A J 8 6 2

This was the bidding when the Spanish ladies were North–South:

South	West	North	East
—	—	3♣[1]	3♠
4♣[2]	5♠	6◇	Dble
6NT[3]	No	No	Dble
End			

[1] Evidently a transfer bid, denoting a solid suit.
[2] At this point 3NT seems the obvious bid.
[3] And now, why remove six diamonds?

West led ♠ 4 against 6 NT. Although many players would do the same, this was a dim effort. Partner's double of six diamonds was surely based on outside tricks and South's 6 NT must mean ♠ A Q.

Declarer won the spade lead with the queen and ran the diamonds, but East was not embarrassed. She came down to ♡ A Q and ♣ K Q, which were bound to produce two tricks.

It is not easy to foresee, but suppose South plays the ace of spades at trick two. Now the endgame becomes tighter:

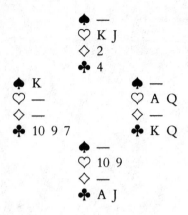

When the last diamond is led from dummy East has no good discard.

At the other table the Italian ladies played in six diamonds doubled, one down, so there was no swing.

The French star, Paul Chemla, is well known for his brilliant and rapid cardplay. One old story about him is worth retelling. A school paid for his teacher's training course at an establishment in Paris, but when the time came for him to take up his duties he received military call-up papers. He wrote to the school to say that he had been called up, and to the army, saying that he had an obligation to teach at the school. Both ploys were successful and he has been a bridge professional ever since. He must do pretty well, for it is said that almost every night he patronizes the top restaurants in Paris – a claim to which his appearance lends support.

Here is one of his many triumphs:

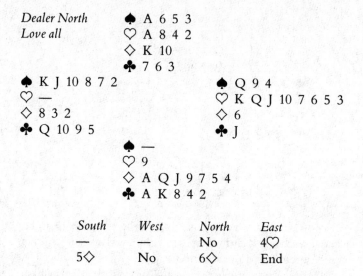

Dealer North
Love all

	♠ A 6 5 3
	♡ A 8 4 2
	◇ K 10
	♣ 7 6 3

♠ K J 10 8 7 2   ♠ Q 9 4
♡ —   ♡ K Q J 10 7 6 5 3
◇ 8 3 2   ◇ 6
♣ Q 10 9 5   ♣ J

	♠ —
	♡ 9
	◇ A Q J 9 7 5 4
	♣ A K 8 4 2

South	West	North	East
—	—	No	4♡
5◇	No	6◇	End

West led a trump against Chemla's six diamonds. Declarer could count eleven top tricks and there would be no problem in establishing a twelfth if clubs broke 3–2. Still, West's failure to lead a heart marked him with a void in that suit and, no doubt, length in both black suits. Chemla's thoughts therefore turned towards a squeeze. He ruffed a low spade at trick 2, crossed to ◇ 10 and ruffed another spade, removing East's guard in the suit.

When all the trumps had been played, this was the ending:

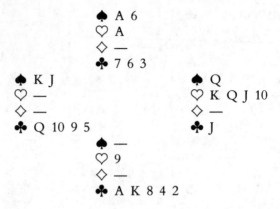

```
            ♠ A 6
            ♡ A
            ◇ —
            ♣ 7 6 3
♠ K J                    ♠ Q
♡ —                      ♡ K Q J 10
◇ —                      ◇ —
♣ Q 10 9 5               ♣ J
            ♠ —
            ♡ 9
            ◇ —
            ♣ A K 8 4 2
```

A heart was played now and West was finished. He chose to throw a club; then declarer played ace and another club and claimed the remainder.

A similar squeeze arose on the next deal, from rubber bridge at the Cavendish Club in New York. Declarer had to work hard for his vulnerable slam.

Dealer North
Game all

```
                    ♠ K 9 6
                    ♡ K 7 6 3 2
                    ◇ A K 6
                    ♣ 10 5
♠ 5                                  ♠ A Q J 10 7 4 3 2
♡ J 5                                ♡ Q 10 9
◇ Q 10 7 5 3 2                       ◇ 4
♣ 9 6 4 3                            ♣ 8
                    ♠ 8
                    ♡ A 8 4
                    ◇ J 9 8
                    ♣ A K Q J 7 2
```

The first problem arose in the bidding. North opened one heart and East overcalled four spades. Trusting partner to hold the ace of diamonds and hoping the heart suit would run, South bid a bold six clubs, which was passed out.

West led ♠ 5, East winning with the 10 and returning the jack. Fearing a singleton on his left, South ruffed with the club ace, and West discarded a diamond.

Dummy's hearts were a disappointment to declarer. Even if he could avoid the loss of a diamond, he would have only eleven tricks on top. The extra trick would have to come from a squeeze, and since he was relying on three tricks from the diamonds the only menace cards he could hope to use were in the major suits. For the squeeze to succeed, both threats would have to lie against the same opponent. It was therefore necessary to assume that East held three hearts as well as the ace of spades.

There were still entry problems. South had to get the diamonds going and run the clubs without disturbing his entry cards in hearts. The first move, while he still had an entry to hand in clubs, was to lead the jack of diamonds. This was covered by the queen and ace. Then came four rounds of trumps, leading to this position:

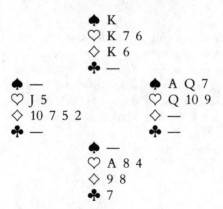

Now a club, followed by two more diamonds, put East on the rack.

If they do everything right, the defenders can just beat the contract. East must return a heart at trick 2, forcing declarer to part with dummy's heart king. When the first diamond is led, West covers, and the entries for the squeeze become unmanageable.

The ancient dodge of ducking a trick to rectify the count often occurs when a *defender* has the lead. Look at this ending, played at notrumps.

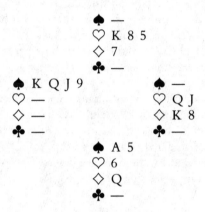

West leads the king of spades and East discards a diamond. If declarer captures, he will score only one more trick – the king of hearts. If declarer ducks, though, East will be squeezed on the next spade lead.

That's the theme of the next deal, played by Patrick Jourdain in a Common Market championship.

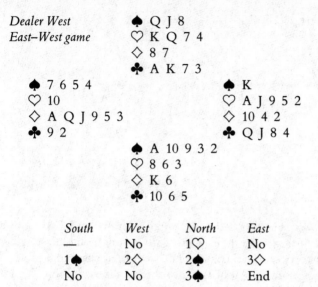

Dealer West   ♠ Q J 8
East–West game   ♡ K Q 7 4
                              ◇ 8 7
                              ♣ A K 7 3

♠ 7 6 5 4   ♠ K
♡ 10   ♡ A J 9 5 2
◇ A Q J 9 5 3   ◇ 10 4 2
♣ 9 2   ♣ Q J 8 4

                              ♠ A 10 9 3 2
                              ♡ 8 6 3
                              ◇ K 6
                              ♣ 10 6 5

South	West	North	East
—	No	1♡	No
1♠	2◇	2♠	3◇
No	No	3♠	End

West led ♡ 10 and dummy's king was allowed to hold. Declarer now played four rounds of trumps. When East parted early on with a heart it was plain that he had begun with five.

After drawing trumps South played a club to the ace and returned a low club, allowing East to win with the jack. Two rounds of diamonds followed, West making the ace and queen. The position was then:

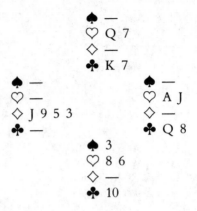

```
              ♠ —
              ♡ Q 7
              ◇ —
              ♣ K 7
♠ —                        ♠ —
♡ —                        ♡ A J
◇ J 9 5 3                  ◇ —
♣ —                        ♣ Q 8
              ♠ 3
              ♡ 8 6
              ◇ —
              ♣ 10
```

West perforce led a diamond, dummy and East both discarding a heart. If South ruffs at this point, East will make two more tricks – the ace of hearts and a club. Suspecting this, Jourdain also threw a heart, leaving West on lead. The next diamond was ruffed and East meanwhile was squeezed in hearts and clubs. This gave declarer the nine tricks he was after.

The ending was certainly unusual, but in reality it was just a variation of the submarine squeeze, where declarer ducks a trick to improve his timing.

The heart situation was similar on the next hand, from the London championship of some years ago. Once again an exceptional ending resulted.

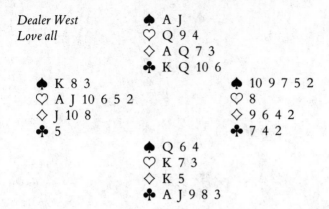

Dealer West
Love all

North
♠ A J
♡ Q 9 4
♢ A Q 7 3
♣ K Q 10 6

West
♠ K 8 3
♡ A J 10 6 5 2
♢ J 10 8
♣ 5

East
♠ 10 9 7 5 2
♡ 8
♢ 9 6 4 2
♣ 7 4 2

South
♠ Q 6 4
♡ K 7 3
♢ K 5
♣ A J 9 8 3

West opened with a weak two hearts and the bidding continued:

South	West	North	East
—	2♡	Dble	No
3NT	No	4NT	No
6NT	End		

West led the jack of diamonds, won by declarer's king. There were eleven tricks on top and on the surface the most likely way to find a twelfth was to play East for a singleton jack or 10 in hearts. However, if South leads the king of hearts early on, West will win and return the jack, destroying any squeeze chances in the major suits.

In practice, the declarer began with a low heart to the queen and eventually arrived at this end position:

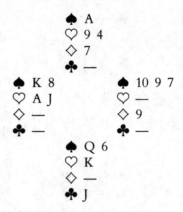

♠ A
♥ 9 4
♦ 7
♣ —

♠ K 8   ♠ 10 9 7
♥ A J   ♥ —
♦ —   ♦ 9
♣ —   ♣ —

♠ Q 6
♥ K
♦ —
♣ J

East had indicated an even number of diamonds, so it seemed that the king of spades was still guarded. Hoping to put West under pressure, declarer played his last club West discarded a spade (best) and dummy a heart. Now the king of spades fell under the ace and dummy exited with a diamond. East suddenly found himself back in the game, forced to concede the last trick to South's queen of spades. A rare jewel in a miniature setting!

Squeezes without the count often end with a throw-in play against the defender whose holdings have been weakened. The next hand, played by Victor Silverstone, led to an unusual position after the throw-in.

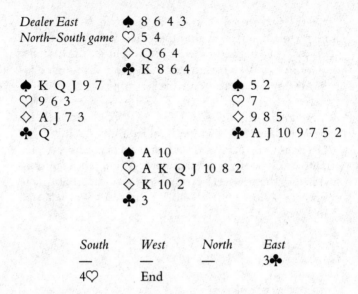

Dealer East
North–South game

	♠ 8 6 4 3	
	♡ 5 4	
	◇ Q 6 4	
	♣ K 8 6 4	
♠ K Q J 9 7		♠ 5 2
♡ 9 6 3		♡ 7
◇ A J 7 3		◇ 9 8 5
♣ Q		♣ A J 10 9 7 5 2
	♠ A 10	
	♡ A K Q J 10 8 2	
	◇ K 10 2	
	♣ 3	

South	West	North	East
—	—	—	3♣
4♡	End		

West led the queen of clubs, which won the first trick. His switch to the king of spades was won by declarer, who proceeded to run the trump suit. West was beginning to scent trouble by the time this end position had been reached:

	♠ 8 6 4	
	♡ —	
	◇ Q 6 4	
	♣ —	
♠ Q J 9		♠ 2
♡ —		♡ —
◇ A J 7		◇ 9 8 5
♣ —		♣ A 10
	♠ 10	
	♡ 8 2	
	◇ K 10 2	
	♣ —	

On the next trump West had to part with ♠ 9. Declarer threw a diamond from dummy, then put West on lead with ♠ J. Leading his other spade would set up a winner in dummy, so West had to exit with a low diamond. This gave declarer two diamond tricks, bringing his total to twelve.

'Should be a good board for us,' West informed his partner. 'Most people would double on my hand.'

No doubt you have noticed that writers on squeeze play tend to dwell on the importance of rectifying the count and maintaining entries. Here is a deal that flouts both these concepts – a no-count, no-entry squeeze. It was reported from a team event in Canada.

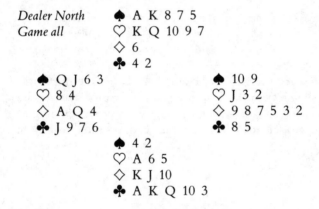

Dealer North
Game all

North:
♠ A K 8 7 5
♡ K Q 10 9 7
◇ 6
♣ 4 2

West:
♠ Q J 6 3
♡ 8 4
◇ A Q 4
♣ J 9 7 6

East:
♠ 10 9
♡ J 3 2
◇ 9 8 7 5 3 2
♣ 8 5

South:
♠ 4 2
♡ A 6 5
◇ K J 10
♣ A K Q 10 3

After North has opened one spade it is sufficient for South to force with three clubs and follow with 3 NT over North's three hearts. However, many players would go too high and it is not surprising that at least one South propelled himself into 6 NT. Although there are only 29 points in the two hands, the contract is not unreasonable, requiring only a favourable break in two of the long suits, clubs and hearts.

With no very attractive lead, West chose a heart. South

discarded a spade on the fourth round of hearts, and this was the position when the fifth heart was led from dummy:

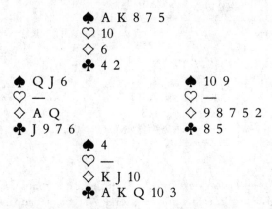

```
              ♠ A K 8 7 5
              ♡ 10
              ◇ 6
              ♣ 4 2
♠ Q J 6                        ♠ 10 9
♡ —                            ♡ —
◇ A Q                          ◇ 9 8 7 5 2
♣ J 9 7 6                      ♣ 8 5
              ♠ 4
              ♡ —
              ◇ K J 10
              ♣ A K Q 10 3
```

What should South discard on the last heart? Obviously not a club, since he hopes to bring in this suit. The diamonds may be needed too, so he parts with ♠ 4, though this is his last communication with dummy.

The spotlight turns on West. Threatened by the extended menace in each black suit, he discards the queen of diamonds. Declarer now cashes one spade, discarding a club. Leaving the other top spade in dignified solitude, he exits with a diamond to the 10 and ace. Whether West exits with a spade or a club, South makes the rest of the tricks. The deal shows what a bad omen it is for one defender to hold all the critical cards.

On the next hand the defender in the West seat, holding a 20-count, might have expected embarrassment in the endgame. Oddly enough, it was his partner who was squeezed. The deal comes from a rubber bridge game at the St James's Club in London, where the standard varies considerably.

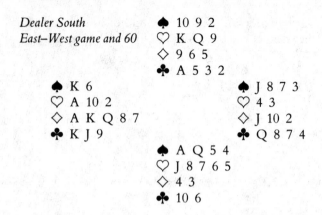

Dealer South
East–West game and 60

	♠ 10 9 2	
	♡ K Q 9	
	◇ 9 6 5	
	♣ A 5 3 2	
♠ K 6		♠ J 8 7 3
♡ A 10 2		♡ 4 3
◇ A K Q 8 7		◇ J 10 2
♣ K J 9		♣ Q 8 7 4
	♠ A Q 5 4	
	♡ J 8 7 6 5	
	◇ 4 3	
	♣ 10 6	

What would you open on the West hand? Perhaps two diamonds, not forcing at the score. Maybe a cautious 1 NT, risking the loss of a slam, or possibly a straight-forward 2 NT. At the table West bid just one diamond and this auction developed:

South	West	North	East
No	1◇	No	1♠
No	2◇	No	No
2♡	2NT	No	3◇
No	No	No	3♡
No	Dble	End	

You might expect West to begin with a high diamond, but no, partner had bid spades and she (does this bring us within the limits of the Act?) began with the king of spades. South won and rather oddly broached the diamond suit. West won and led a second spade, covered by the jack and ace. After a heart to the king declarer led another diamond. West, seemingly not interested in a spade ruff, overtook her partner's 10 and played a third round of diamonds, on which South discarded a club. After ace of clubs, a club ruff, and a heart to West's ace, the position was:

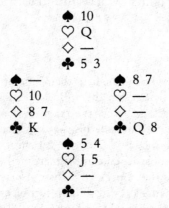

```
                ♠ 10
                ♡ Q
                ◇ —
                ♣ 5 3
    ♠ —                       ♠ 8 7
    ♡ 10                      ♡ —
    ◇ 8 7                     ◇ —
    ♣ K                       ♣ Q 8
                ♠ 5 4
                ♡ J 5
                ◇ —
                ♣ —
```

Now West launched ♡ 10, catching her partner in a trump squeeze. Contract made.

'Nicely played, partner,' said North.

'Extraordinary,' said West. 'I had 20 points. It wasn't wrong to double, was it?'

9

Hands bizarre and macabre

Television channels schedule their horror films late at night, hoping that all but the most determined infants will then be well asleep. We have taken a similarly cautious approach with the hands in this chapter, leaving them until the very end of the book. Anyone still with us at this stage will surely be a hardened campaigner, well accustomed to the cruel tricks that a pack of cards can play.

We'll start with a small bidding problem. Your right-hand opponent, vulnerable, opens a 15–17 notrump. What move do you make on:

♠ A 7 2
♥ A
♦ A Q 9 8 5 4 3 2
♣ 9

Is there much point in doubling? And if you decide to bid diamonds, how many? Five diamonds might be a silly contract, and partner is unlikely to be able to raise four diamonds – he won't expect you to be so strong. Since the opponents are vulnerable, it might be clever to pass and hope for an easy 300 or so.

The player who originally held these cards decided to double and found a surprisingly good hand opposite. This was the deal:

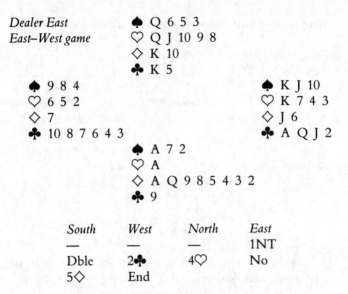

Dealer East
East–West game

		♠ Q 6 5 3	
		♡ Q J 10 9 8	
		◇ K 10	
		♣ K 5	
♠ 9 8 4			♠ K J 10
♡ 6 5 2			♡ K 7 4 3
◇ 7			◇ J 6
♣ 10 8 7 6 4 3			♣ A Q J 2
		♠ A 7 2	
		♡ A	
		◇ A Q 9 8 5 4 3 2	
		♣ 9	

South	West	North	East
—	—	—	1NT
Dble	2♣	4♡	No
5◇	End		

West led ♣ 6, a singularly feeble choice, and the king of clubs lost to the ace. When the queen of clubs was returned, South ruffed and led a number of diamonds.

East had to be careful with his discards now. If he came down to ♠ K J 10 ♡ K or ♠ K J ♡ K 7 he could be endplayed. West helped his partner by discarding all three hearts and East was then able to keep ♠ K J ♡ K ♣ J, beating the game by one trick.

The play was discussed at some length and finally East was able to tell declarer how he might have made the contract. 'Instead of ruffing the second club,' he said, 'you should discard the ace of hearts! Then I'm endplayed. I have to give you an extra entry to the dummy and you can take the ruffing finesse in hearts.'

'In that case I'm surprised you continued with clubs,' declared South, retrieving some dignity from the situation. 'Return a diamond or a heart and I've no chance.'

One eight-card suit deserves another. There were two of

them on this deal, from an international trial in Australia.

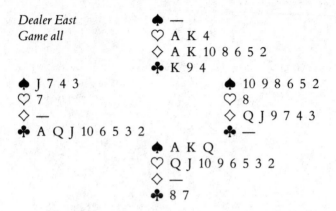

Dealer East
Game all

♠ —
♡ A K 4
◇ A K 10 8 6 5 2
♣ K 9 4

♠ J 7 4 3
♡ 7
◇ —
♣ A Q J 10 6 5 3 2

♠ 10 9 8 6 5 2
♡ 8
◇ Q J 9 7 4 3
♣ —

♠ A K Q
♡ Q J 10 9 6 5 3 2
◇ —
♣ 8 7

There was a large field and it seems that every possible misfortune occurred at one table or another.

If South opens one heart and West overcalls five clubs, what do you think North should bid? There is a good case for 6 NT. Partner, with nothing much in clubs, must hold the top spades. Some North players were content to double five clubs, settling for a safe 800. Other Norths, hoping for better things, tried six diamonds. Now, if East passes as though going to his own funeral, should South continue to six hearts? Most players would, no doubt, but six hearts can be defeated by ace and another club.

At one table East was foolish enough to double six diamonds. South bid six hearts and East doubled again. Now North tried 6 NT, reaching the top spot at last. East, as players will, doubled a third time and North claimed thirteen tricks after the opening lead

At some tables – though it is difficult to imagine the bidding – East–West found a 'sacrifice' in six spades. It wasn't cheap; generally 1,700 after South had begun with the top spades.

We still haven't mentioned the most traumatic result of

all, one that is said to have occurred more than once. Put yourself in the West seat, defending six hearts doubled. You make the daring lead of ♣ 2 and – oh joy – partner ruffs and returns a diamond. 'The rest are mine,' says South, ruffing high.

There was nothing wrong with East's double on the next hand. It was the ensuing defence that led to all the arguments.

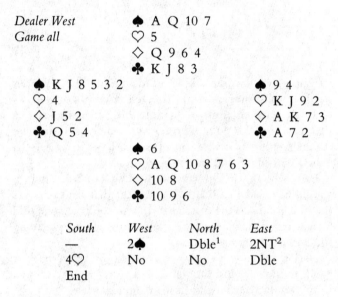

Dealer West
Game all

```
              ♠ A Q 10 7
              ♡ 5
              ◇ Q 9 6 4
              ♣ K J 8 3
♠ K J 8 5 3 2                  ♠ 9 4
♡ 4                            ♡ K J 9 2
◇ J 5 2                        ◇ A K 7 3
♣ Q 5 4                        ♣ A 7 2
              ♠ 6
              ♡ A Q 10 8 7 6 3
              ◇ 10 8
              ♣ 10 9 6
```

South	West	North	East
—	2♠	Dble[1]	2NT[2]
4♡	No	No	Dble
End			

[1] It's usual to play takeout doubles over weak twos. North–South had evidently not discussed their methods.
[2] Pointless, whatever the meaning of North's double.

West, with a difficult lead, was out of luck when he tried a spade. Declarer finessed the queen and discarded a diamond on the ace. A heart to the 10 was followed by the 6 of clubs to dummy's 8. East won with the ace and the position was now:

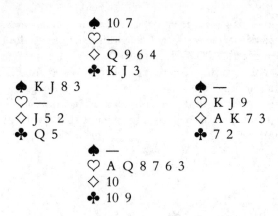

```
                    ♠ 10 7
                    ♡ —
                    ◇ Q 9 6 4
                    ♣ K J 3
♠ K J 8 3                          ♠ —
♡ —                                ♡ K J 9
◇ J 5 2                            ◇ A K 7 3
♣ Q 5                              ♣ 7 2
                    ♠ —
                    ♡ A Q 8 7 6 3
                    ◇ 10
                    ♣ 10 9
```

East played ace and king of diamonds and declarer, needing no further assistance, moved smoothly on his way towards a triple trump reduction. He ruffed the second diamond and crossed to dummy twice in clubs to ruff two more diamonds. Down to just three cards – ♡ A Q 8 – he exited with the 8 and made the contract.

East, who (a) should have allowed ♣ 8 to hold, and (b) should have led a club after cashing the diamond ace, was the first to unsheathe his claws. It was your fault, he told his partner, you should have blocked the clubs by playing the queen on the first round!

Declarer ran into an even worse trump break on the next hand. Curiously, his only chance to recover was to find a similarly untoward break in his main side suit.

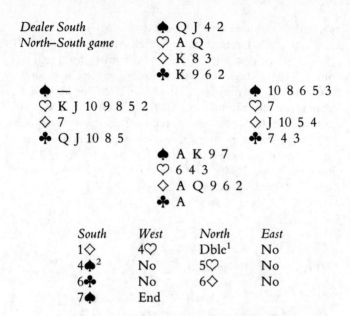

Dealer South
North–South game

	♠ Q J 4 2	
	♡ A Q	
	◇ K 8 3	
	♣ K 9 6 2	

♠ —		♠ 10 8 6 5 3
♡ K J 10 9 8 5 2		♡ 7
◇ 7		◇ J 10 5 4
♣ Q J 10 8 5		♣ 7 4 3

	♠ A K 9 7	
	♡ 6 4 3	
	◇ A Q 9 6 2	
	♣ A	

South	West	North	East
1◇	4♡	Dble[1]	No
4♠[2]	No	5♡	No
6♣	No	6◇	No
7♠	End		

[1] North declared afterwards that his double was 'forward-looking'!

[2] The next three bids were all control-showing, spades being the agreed suit.

The queen of clubs was led, won in the South hand. When declarer played the ace of trumps a shock was in store for him. West, trying hard not to look pleased, showed out. Now the only chance was to make four diamond tricks, discarding a heart from dummy. After that, a cross-ruff might operate.

Declarer crossed to the king of diamonds and, with the touch of a showman, returned the 3 to his 6. West showed out and declarer cashed two more rounds of diamonds, discarding the queen of hearts from dummy. After cashing the ace of hearts and the king of clubs, he made the remainder on a cross-ruff. His last two losers in the red suits were ruffed with dummy's high trumps.

It is strange that a heart lead would probably beat the contract. If declarer starts with the ace of spades, as before, then turns to diamonds, East should split his diamond honours on the second round. There would then be no convenient entry to dummy to repeat the diamond finesse.

On now to an exotic opening lead problem from an American Lifemasters Pairs. You will need to know a bit about the rules of the game to come up with the right answer. You are West, holding these cards:

♠ 8 6 3
♡ 6
♢ A K 5 4 2
♣ 10 9 6 4

This has been the bidding:

South	West	North	East
—	—	1♠	2♢
2♡	No	3♣	No
3♢	5♢	5♡	No
6♡	End		

Your partner had incapably dropped the ace of clubs on the table just before the auction, so you were barred from the bidding on the first round. Now you are on lead, and the declarer, exercising one of his options, prohibits a club lead. What do you do?

This was the full deal:

```
              ♠ A Q 7 5 4
              ♡ J 5
              ◇ 6
              ♣ K Q 7 5 3
♠ 8 6 3                        ♠ J 9
♡ 6                            ♡ 7 4 3
◇ A K 5 4 2                    ◇ Q J 10 9 8 3
♣ 10 9 6 4                     ♣ A J
              ♠ K 10 2
              ♡ A K Q 10 9 8 2
              ◇ 7
              ♣ 8 2
```

West, one of America's top stars, led a low diamond at
trick one! His heart sank when a lowly 8 appeared from
partner, but all was well. East cashed the ace of clubs to
defeat the contract. You see why it was essential to under-
lead the ace-king? The prohibition against leading a club
exists so long as the lead is retained. If West had led a top
diamond he would not have been allowed to lead a club at
trick 2, and then South's club losers would vanish into the
night on dummy's spade suit.

Staying with opening leads, see what you make of this
one. You hold:

              ♠ A 10 9
              ♡ A Q 8 5
              ◇ K Q 2
              ♣ A 7 3

You are West and the bidding goes:

South	West	North	East
—	—	No	No
1♠	1NT	3♠	4♡
4♠	No	No	Dble
End			

The question is not so much 'What should West lead?' as 'Is there any conceivable reason for leading a low club?' For this is a hand with a history. Two Indonesian brothers, named Manoppo, were at that time under a small-cloud following their win in the Far Eastern Championship. This incident was widely quoted, for partner held:

♠ J
♡ 9 6 4 3 2
♢ 10 8 7 5 3
♣ K 9

Obviously West's lead of a low club was an outstanding success.

José Le Dentu, writing in the French magazine *Le Bridgeur*, went over the top in his commentary. 'Is there really one expert in all the world capable of finding such a lead unless he had a secret code with his partner?' he wrote; and 'it is evident that this hand alone would suffice to convince a jury'.

But if the bidding is correctly recorded, what is West to make of East's double of four spades? He can't have anything worth while in trumps, nor would he place much value on the king of hearts, his long suit. If he holds the ace of diamonds, which is unlikely, there is no hurry to play on that suit. If, much more likely, his double is based on club values, then it may be essential to attack that suit straightaway. A low club lead could gain in several cases, not just when East holds ♣ K x. It might work well opposite Q x (x) or Q J (x), for example. Also, if East holds ♣ K x x or ♣ K x x x it may be essential for him to win the first club, so that he can lead a diamond through declarer's ace.

The problem of the lead was posed a few years later in the (American) *Bridge World's* bidding competition. The panel voted like this:

♠ 10   20 votes
♡ A   7 votes
♠ A   4 votes
♢ K   3 votes
♡ 8   1 vote

Leading ♡ 8 is not such a bad idea. As with a low club lead, it might give partner a chance to lead a diamond through the ace, aiding the defence. Still, it wasn't so bright for the panel to overlook altogether the merit of a low club.

Another amazing club lead (no suspicions were attached to this one) was found in a world championship clash between Italy and a new zone bearing the cumbersome title of Central–American–Caribbean. This was the deal:

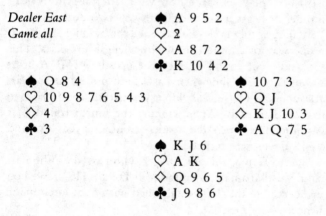

Dealer East
Game all

	♠ A 9 5 2	
	♡ 2	
	♢ A 8 7 2	
	♣ K 10 4 2	
♠ Q 8 4		♠ 10 7 3
♡ 10 9 8 7 6 5 4 3		♡ Q J
♢ 4		♢ K J 10 3
♣ 3		♣ A Q 7 5
	♠ K J 6	
	♡ A K	
	♢ Q 9 6 5	
	♣ J 9 8 6	

When Italy was North–South the bidding went:

South	West	North	East
De Falco	Dhers	Franco	Calvo
—	—	—	No
1◇	No	1♠	No
1NT	No	2◇	No
2♡	No	3♣	No
3NT	End		

Possessing little confidence in his long heart suit, West led his singleton club. East won with the queen and switched to the queen of hearts. South cleared the clubs and East led another heart.

With no picture of the heart distribution, De Falco decided to play on spades. So West, after all, did make a number of heart tricks and South was two down.

At all the other tables East opened the bidding and West, in one way or another, showed his length in hearts. This put a different complexion on the play in 3 NT. A heart was usually led, and when East could not return a heart after winning the second club it was natural for declarer to play on diamonds. After winning the fourth round East was forced to open the spades. South played low and West's queen was trapped.

Alberto Calvo, the only player who passed on the East hand, was Panama's ambassador in Tokyo. He showed on this occasion the long-established virtue of diplomatic silence.

A club lead would have been just the thing on the next deal, too, from a European Championship match between Britain and Spain. It was an unusual hand; declarer's best chance of success was to find a 5–0 trump break against him!

Dealer South
East–West game

```
            ♠ —
            ♡ A K 6 3
            ◇ A Q 8 4
            ♣ A K Q 9 8
♠ A Q J 8 5 3                    ♠ —
♡ Q 8 5 2                        ♡ J 10 4
◇ K J 9                          ◇ 10 7 6 5 2
♣ —                              ♣ 7 6 5 4 2
            ♠ K 10 9 7 6 4 2
            ♡ 9 7
            ◇ 3
            ♣ J 10 3
```

South	West	North	East
Hackett	Cabot	Collings	Maso
1♣[1]	Dble	No[2]	1◇
No	1♠	2♠	No
3♣[3]	No	3♠	No
3NT[4]	No	4◇[5]	No
4♠[6]	No	6♣	End

[1] They were playing a method in which an opening one club might be genuine, might be 0–8 (a pass normally indicated 9–12).

[2] Waiting in the undergrowth.

[3] In principle a 4-card suit – but he hadn't got one, apart from spades. He must have thought of passing two spades, but could not be sure of sympathetic understanding should this turn out to be the wrong move.

[4] I have the spades stopped, partner.

[5] Asking bid in diamonds.

[6] Second-round diamond control.

West, trumpless, led the ace of spades and declarer rattled off twelve tricks by way of four red-suit winners and eight trumps scored separately. Had North played the hand, East would surely have led a trump, leaving declarer one trick short.

In the other room the British West opened one spade and North doubled. The Spanish South, failing to visualize a slam in his direction, passed the double and collected 500. That was a swing of 9 IMPs to Britain.

One supposedly guaranteed way of getting the lead you want is the Lightner double. It was used at both tables on the next deal, from the play-off for the American women's Olympiad team, but misfired badly at one of them.

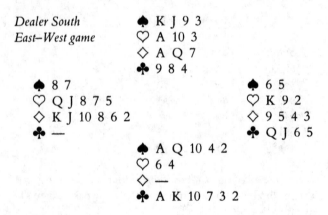

Dealer South
East–West game

♠ K J 9 3
♡ A 10 3
♢ A Q 7
♣ 9 8 4

♠ 8 7
♡ Q J 8 7 5
♢ K J 10 8 6 2
♣ —

♠ 6 5
♡ K 9 2
♢ 9 5 4 3
♣ Q J 6 5

♠ A Q 10 4 2
♡ 6 4
♢ —
♣ A K 10 7 3 2

This was the bidding at the first table:

South	West	North	East
Moss	Keller	Mitchell	Peterson
1♣	2NT[1]	3NT[2]	No
4♢[3]	Dble[4]	Rdble	No
4♠	No	5♡	No
6♣	No	6♠	No
7♠[5]	Dble[6]	End	

[1] Such two-suited overcalls are usually more helpful to the

opponents than to the defending side. On weak hands they are foolish.

2 Much more sensible than a double.

3 Too good for an immediate four spades.

4 Pointless. It merely extends the options open to North.

5 Partner had shown the ace of hearts and her own black suits were fairly strong.

6 The sort of miscalculation that can occur at the end of a long match – and a long sequence. West forgets that she is on lead herself.

Drawing the right conclusion from West's final double, Gail Moss took the deep finesse in clubs and made the contract. They reached the grand at the other table too:

South	West	North	East
1♣	No	1♠	No
4♢	No	4NT	No
5♡	No	6♠	No
7♠	Dble	End	

This time the double was successful: East led a club and West ruffed. The North–South pair were left to wonder whether they might have believed the double and transferred to 7NT, which presumably they would have made.

One of the most annoying situations in the game occurs when you are up against a declarer who seems to misplay hand after hand, yet always lands on his feet. The declarer on the next deal took several wrong turns during the play of a single hand, but he still survived till near the finish.

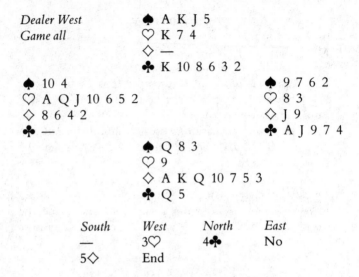

Dealer West   ♠ A K J 5
Game all   ♡ K 7 4
                ♢ —
                ♣ K 10 8 6 3 2

♠ 10 4   ♠ 9 7 6 2
♡ A Q J 10 6 5 2   ♡ 8 3
♢ 8 6 4 2   ♢ J 9
♣ —   ♣ A J 9 7 4

                ♠ Q 8 3
                ♡ 9
                ♢ A K Q 10 7 5 3
                ♣ Q 5

South	West	North	East
—	3♡	4♣	No
5♢	End		

West began with the ace and queen of hearts and declarer faced his first problem: should he play the king or ruff in hand? At first it may look right to ruff in hand, play off the trumps, and turn to spades if the jack of diamonds doesn't fall in three rounds. However, this is not necessarily correct, because unless the defender with four diamonds holds four spades declarer may still not be able to dispose of his clubs in time. It is therefore better to take the king of hearts while this card is not likely to be ruffed.

Following this line, South rose with the heart king and discarded a club. The next question was how to cross to hand. A spade, you say? No, declarer didn't fancy this. He played a heart instead.

East ruffed with the diamond jack and it seems obvious now for declarer to discard his second club. This would have been fatal as the cards lie, though, because a club from East would then promote West's ♢ 8. Fortunately for declarer, the play never occurred to him. He overruffed and drew three rounds of trumps, arriving at this position:

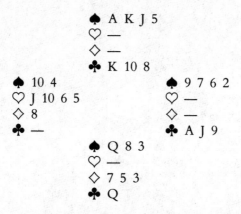

```
                    ♠ A K J 5
                    ♡ —
                    ◇ —
                    ♣ K 10 8
    ♠ 10 4                         ♠ 9 7 6 2
    ♡ J 10 6 5                     ♡ —
    ◇ 8                            ◇ —
    ♣ —                            ♣ A J 9
                    ♠ Q 8 3
                    ♡ —
                    ◇ 7 5 3
                    ♣ Q
```

Now our hero played on spades, hoping that three rounds would stand up and he would be able to discard his second club loser in time. A hopeless line, of course, because West had already shown seven hearts and four diamonds, so could not hold three spades. If South simply exits with a diamond he still makes the contract, because West is void in clubs. Whether West would then have been able to steel himself to say 'Well played' is another matter.

Declarer certainly deserved such a plaudit on the next deal. He held A x opposite x x in a side suit and the only way of making the contract was by ruffing the ace! Impossible, you think? Well, look at this deal:

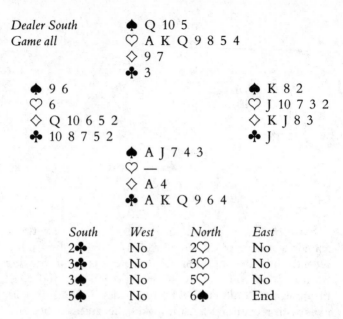

Dealer South   ♠ Q 10 5
Game all   ♡ A K Q 9 8 5 4
            ♢ 9 7
            ♣ 3

♠ 9 6   ♠ K 8 2
♡ 6   ♡ J 10 7 3 2
♢ Q 10 6 5 2   ♢ K J 8 3
♣ 10 8 7 5 2   ♣ J

            ♠ A J 7 4 3
            ♡ —
            ♢ A 4
            ♣ A K Q 9 6 4

South	West	North	East
2♣	No	2♡	No
3♣	No	3♡	No
3♠	No	5♡	No
5♠	No	6♠	End

West led his singleton heart and South discarded a diamond. The queen of spades held the next trick and declarer followed with a low spade to the jack, leaving East with the king.

At this point most declarers would cash the ace of clubs and ruff a club, blaming the weather when East overruffed and they had to give up another trick in clubs.

It's not the right play, though. After the jack of spades has held, it cannot be wrong to follow with the ace and king of clubs. It does East no good to ruff (South will ruff one club and discard two) and he should hold off again when the queen of clubs is played. The position is then:

134

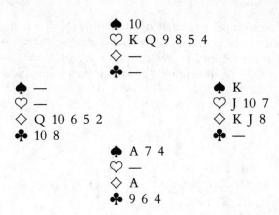

```
              ♠ 10
              ♡ K Q 9 8 5 4
              ◇ —
              ♣ —
♠ —                        ♠ K
♡ —                        ♡ J 10 7
◇ Q 10 6 5 2               ◇ K J 8
♣ 10 8                     ♣ —
              ♠ A 7 4
              ♡ —
              ◇ A
              ♣ 9 6 4
```

The great moment has arrived. Declarer ruffs the ace of diamonds and discards two clubs on ♡ K Q, losing just one club at the finish.

If you think the deal had the air of a composition about it, what about this next one? It was reported as coming from actual play in Bucharest and appeared a very likely contender for one of the Bols brilliancy awards.

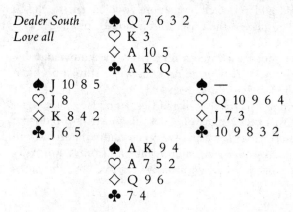

```
Dealer South      ♠ Q 7 6 3 2
Love all          ♡ K 3
                  ◇ A 10 5
                  ♣ A K Q
♠ J 10 8 5                      ♠ —
♡ J 8                           ♡ Q 10 9 6 4
◇ K 8 4 2                       ◇ J 7 3
♣ J 6 5                         ♣ 10 9 8 3 2
                  ♠ A K 9 4
                  ♡ A 7 5 2
                  ◇ Q 9 6
                  ♣ 7 4
```

South played in six spades and West, we are told, led the jack of hearts. Declarer won in dummy and drew three rounds of trumps, followed by three top clubs. On the third club declarer made a sensational play – instead of throwing a diamond, he ruffed. After ace of hearts and a heart ruff, West discarding a diamond, the position was:

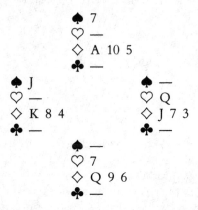

```
              ♠ 7
              ♡ —
              ◇ A 10 5
              ♣ —
  ♠ J                        ♠ —
  ♡ —                        ♡ Q
  ◇ K 8 4                    ◇ J 7 3
  ♣ —                        ♣ —
              ♠ —
              ♡ 7
              ◇ Q 9 6
              ♣ —
```

When ♠ 7 was led from dummy, East had to keep the queen of hearts and therefore threw a diamond. West won the spade and returned a diamond, which ran to the 9. South then played the queen of diamonds, pinning East's jack.

Clever; but then came a note from the knowledgeable editor of the IBPA *Bulletin*, recalling a *very* similar problem set by the late Paul Lukacs in 1980.

Lightning can strike twice in the same place, of course. An almost exact replica of a scintillating trump-reducing coup described in *Reese on Play* was recently reported from Australia. A somewhat sour comment from a normally tolerant author was vigorously rejected by the anti-podeans.